SPIRIT
WARS

SPIRIT WARS

WINNING THE INVISIBLE BATTLE AGAINST SIN AND THE ENEMY

KRIS VALLOTTON

Chosen

a division of Baker Publishing Group
Minneapolis, Minnesota

© 2012 by Kris Vallotton

Published by Chosen Books
11400 Hampshire Avenue South
Bloomington, MN 55438
www.chosenbooks.com

Chosen Books is a division of
Baker Publishing Group, Grand Rapids, Michigan.

Printed in the United States of America

Library of Congress Cataloging-in-Publication Data
Vallotton, Kris.
    Spirit wars : winning the invisible battle against sin and the enemy / Kris Vallotton ; foreword by Bill Johnson.
        p.   cm.
    Includes bibliographical references (p. 205).
    ISBN 978-0-8007-9493-4 (pbk. : alk. paper)
    1. Spiritual warfare. I. Title.
BV4509.5.V35 2012
235′.4—dc23   2011036926

The Internet addresses, email addresses and phone numbers in this book are accurate at the time of publication. They are provided as a resource. Baker Publishing Group does not endorse them or vouch for their content or permanence.

Cover design by Kirk DouPonce, DogEared Design

12   13   14   15   16   17   7   6   5

I dedicate this work to every person who is bound in a spiritual prison, longing to be free and fighting for peace. May you find rest for your souls, peace for your minds and joy for your hearts as you journey through the pages of this book.

Contents

Foreword

My wife and I have been friends with Kris and Kathy Vallotton and their children for over 32 years. They are two of the most important people in our lives. Our children grew up together. We simply have lived life together. In fact, for a season, they lived with us until their home was built. I watched *Spirit Wars* unfold. What you hold in your hands is the farthest thing from *theory* that you could imagine. It is real, sobering and promising, taken from a life trained in the trenches. As much as I would like to promote the "happily ever after" lifestyle, I am reminded that we were born into a war—a war that has already been won.

Kris is known for his incredible prophetic ministry. And rightly so. The impact is now international. I stand amazed at the open doors and the boldness Kris has to go into impossible situations and bring change for the glory of God. He is also known for power in ministry. It really does not matter if it is healing or deliverance needed; he ministers well in both. He is also recognized all over the world as an extremely capable preacher of the Gospel of the Kingdom. The impact of his teaching gift will be measured only in eternity. But I think both heaven and hell know his name for another reason altogether, one that only those closest to him would see. Heaven and hell both see that no matter what the circumstances are, Kris Vallotton believes God. He is truly a friend of God.

Watching this story unfold was fun at times and painful at other times. Yet I cannot help but think of the well-known passage in Romans in this regard: "For I consider that the sufferings of this present time are not worthy to be compared with the glory that is to be revealed to us" (Romans 8:18). The victories that have followed Kris, both for their family and through their ministry, have put the pain involved in its rightful place—squarely under Kris's feet.

Kris has written many books, all of which have brought life, identity and insight to great numbers of people. But I do not think I have ever been more excited about one of his books than I am about this one. On many occasions, people have come to me needing help and insight for their unusual spiritual struggles. Those struggles often remind me of Kris's story. I have encouraged people to get a copy of Kris's testimony on CD, because those who listen to it are changed. But as good as the CD is, this book is much more complete. It captures the heart of the issue when it comes to spiritual conflict in a way that one CD could never touch. Plus, it can be used as a manual and read over and over again.

Even though Kris is a close friend, I would not be nearly as excited as I am about his ministry and this book if he glorified warfare and created a devil consciousness. But I have watched his life. He refuses, no matter what has happened, to set his eyes on his enemy. They are on Jesus, the author and finisher of his faith—our faith.

It has been said that often prophets' lives are parables. They go through things that bring a message to the Body of Christ. If that is true, and I believe it is, then Kris's freedom will bring exponential increase for the glory of God because what the enemy meant for evil, God has turned around for good. The delivered is a deliverer!

It is with great excitement that I recommend this book to you, knowing that fruit will increase until Jesus gets His full reward.

Bill Johnson
Author, *When Heaven Invades Earth*
and *Face to Face with God*
Senior Pastor, Bethel Church, Redding, California

Acknowledgments

Kathy, thank you for all the hard years you stood by me when I was struggling to find my way out of spiritual bondage. Thank you for all the times you woke up in the middle of the night to pray for me. Thank you for believing in me when I was really broken. And most of all, thank you for loving me all our lives.

Introduction

I have written six books prior to this one. Whenever you submit a manuscript to publishers, one of the first questions they ask is, What qualifies you to write this book? I am sure they are hoping for some letters after your name, or an Ivy League degree. But I was inspired to write this book out of my own experience with the demonic realm. As a young Christian, I spent over three years being very demonized. I have a Ph.D. in fear, oppression and anxiety, which makes this the most difficult book I have ever written.

The struggle is not that I do not know what I am talking about; the real problem is that I do! Writing this book has required me to recall some of the worst experiences of my life. Nevertheless, I made a covenant with the Lord the day He delivered me that I would spend my life helping others find freedom. Consequently, over the past three decades I have helped literally thousands of captives and prisoners go free. But three years ago, something happened that caused me to become even more vigilant. My own daughter, and later my son, came under a demonic attack that nearly destroyed them both and threatened to take out our entire family. In the midst of this intense battle, I decided that I would never again let someone else's daughter, son, father or mother be destroyed while I stood by and watched. My prayer and my goal is that through this book, millions of people will become equipped to make a prison break and destroy the works of the devil on their way out of the POW camp.

Ignorance Is Bliss?

Many say that ignorance is bliss, but God says, "My people are destroyed for lack of knowledge" (Hosea 4:6). I am astonished by how many people (including Christians) are unaware that we do not inhabit, but we cohabit, this planet. The apostle Paul began to unveil this mystery to us when he wrote, "Now concerning spiritual gifts, brethren, I do not want you to be unaware" (1 Corinthians 12:1). The word *gifts* here does not appear in the original Greek text. The verse actually should read, "Now concerning the spiritual, brethren, I do not want you to be unaware." Then Paul goes on to use the gifts of the Spirit as an example of how the spirit realm functions.

Although Christians typically acknowledge this unseen realm on some intellectual level, I personally do not think they really believe that the spirit world has an effect on their daily lives. Teaching some people about the spirit world feels very much like trying to convince someone in the 1800s that there really was such a thing as germs, and that these germs could make them sick or even kill them. Over the last two centuries, medical and technological discoveries advanced our understanding of this previously unseen natural realm and saved millions of lives.

Much like the transition that took place with medical breakthroughs in the natural, a transition is now taking place in the spiritual. Society has become increasingly hungry to understand the spirit realm. Angels and demons have rapidly become the subject of many books and movies. It seems as though the invisible dimensions of life, which constantly reach through the veil of the unexplainable, fascinate the entire world. Books and movies like *Harry Potter* and *Lord of the Rings* are contemporary examples of the hunger people have to comprehend and participate in this dimension. It is imperative that we understand the effects that angels and demons can have on our personal lives, or we can become victims of the invisible world. Paul wrote, "You were dead in your trespasses and sins, in which you formerly walked according to the course of this world, according to the prince of the power of the air, of the spirit that is now working in the sons of disobedience" (Ephesians 2:1–2). In other words, before we knew Jesus, we were literally the puppets of demonic spirits.

Many people in First World countries have a hard time imagining that there is a "prince of the power of the air" controlling the thoughts of everyday people. The idea that the world is inhabited by invisible beings is, to them, a metaphor or even a fairy tale like Santa Claus or the Easter Bunny. People in developing nations, on the other hand, have no problem believing in a spirit realm because the effects of demons are so overt. Witch doctors, medicine men and voodoo priests dominate their cultures to the point that nearly everyone who lives in such a place has experienced the demonic realm firsthand.

Freedom Fighters

When we think about people fighting for freedom from evil spirits, we often envision a primitive warrior slithering on the ground in a mud hut in the middle of a jungle somewhere. But my own experience has convinced me that evil spirits are just as influential in First World countries as they are in developing nations like Africa—they just manifest differently. We may not have many witch doctors or voodoo priests in the United States, for instance, but people are just as demonized in "the land of the free and the home of the brave" as elsewhere. Understanding how to dispel demons and dispatch angels can make the difference between living a joy-filled life and becoming a captive of some evil scheme.

You may be thinking that I am a "demon under every rock" kind of guy. *I am not!* I must admit, though, that when I first got free from years of bondage, I absolutely went through that season. I think that as you read this book, however, you will find that I take a very balanced approach to life in its pages. I worked hard to weigh my experience, the counsel of mental and medical health professionals, and the Word of God as I wrote each chapter. As you learn more from this book about how to win the invisible battle against sin and the enemy, I hope you find freedom and joy in its pages.

1

Fighting for Peace

In 1975, I finally married the woman of my dreams. I had waited five long years for her.

I met Kathy when she was twelve (I was fifteen), floating on a raft in the middle of a lake. We were engaged by the time she was thirteen! Kathy's folks forbade us to marry until she finished high school, so she took extra classes and worked really hard to graduate a year early. Waiting all those years to get married was torture. To make matters worse, we lived thirty miles apart, so we only saw each other on the weekends. I would arrive on Friday and stay at Kathy's parents' house. As I left for home each Sunday, Kathy would stand in the middle of the street and cry while waving good-bye. During the week, we spent hours on the phone every day, often talking halfway through the night. Hours seemed like days and days felt like months as we longed to begin our life together.

I graduated from Sunnyvale High School in Sunnyvale, California, in 1973. The Carpenters' song "We've Only Just

Begun" was a big hit that year, and it was the theme of our senior yearbook. It also became a prophetic declaration over Kathy and me, as we both became Christians a few months before I graduated. We found God in the Jesus movement, and we both had powerful conversion experiences. We were so excited about our faith.

Our wedding day finally arrived on a warm summer day in July. With three hundred people looking on, we repeated our vows and kissed way too long while everyone cheered. Our ship was finally launched into what would prove to be the high seas of a great love affair. Unlike many marriages, our first year together was like heaven on earth. It seemed as though all we did was play, explore each other and laugh a lot. I had a job as an automotive technician managing a repair shop in the Bay Area, and Kathy was our bookkeeper. Together we made a pretty good living, and soon we were able to buy a new house. I preferred that we wait awhile to have children, but Kathy wanted to have them right away, and she kept prodding me as only a wife can do. In a weak moment she got the best of me, and soon she was pregnant with our first child.

A Time to Mourn

Then suddenly, the season changed and our tiny ship encountered a huge storm that would almost sink us. It began with Kathy's pregnancy, which made her incredibly sick. She vomited about fifty times a day and lost weight through the eighth month of her pregnancy. She could hardly get off the couch.

While Kathy was fighting her way through pregnancy, I was carrying tons of responsibility at the shop. Managing thirteen people when I was twenty years old was extremely challenging. I worked twelve hours a day, six days a week and rarely stopped to eat lunch. Consequently, my diet consisted mostly of candy bars, Coke and potato chips.

One night, exhausted from a long, hard week of work, I got in the bathtub to relax my tired body while Kathy lay sick on the sofa. An hour or so later, I started to get out of the tub to dry off. But as I stood up, an *intense* thought hit me: *I am going to die!*

Like everyone else in the world, bad thoughts were not foreign to me, but this was different. This thought was so strong that it caused panic to rush through my whole being like stampeding cattle! My entire body trembled, my heart pounded out of my chest and my pulse raced uncontrollably. All my strength drained from my limbs, and I struggled to get out of the tub. I fell back into the water, shouting desperately for Kathy to help me. Eight months pregnant, she labored to get up off the couch. She rushed into the bathroom where I lay helpless and scared, white as a ghost. I could barely talk, but I managed to mumble something about having a heart attack. She strained to help me out of the bathtub and onto the couch. Then she ran into the kitchen to call our family doctor, who was a customer of ours at the auto shop. He relayed a few questions to me through Kathy and concluded that I was having a *panic attack*, not a heart attack. Little did I know that this was the beginning of a three-and-a-half-year journey through hell.

Touring Hell and Calling for Heaven

That first panic attack initiated a constant state of fear in me. Going to work became really tough. It took all the strength I could muster just to get out of bed each morning. All through the day at the shop, high levels of anxiety overwhelmed my soul like waves crashing on the seashore in a violent storm. It was everything I could do just to concentrate on my job. As difficult as the days were, nights were much worse. The panic attacks continued, turning into endless, tormenting nightmares. Horrible images filled my mind as I imagined terrible things happening to me or envisioned myself performing dreadful acts. Although I knew in my heart that these images and thoughts were illusions, they still *felt* so real. I often wondered if I were losing my mind. I could not sleep much, and I soaked the sheets with sweat every night.

A few months into my ordeal, our daughter Jaime was born. Kathy and I were so excited about our first child, but the added stress of the baby intensified my battle. Kathy was amazing through it all. Getting up several times a night to take care of the baby or to comfort me was more than most women could take, but Kathy was rarely shaken. I can only conclude that God had given her a special grace for the battle. She was a solace in the storm, a force of peace in a very troubled situation.

A year passed without any relief. Finally, Kathy and I decided to quit our jobs and move up into the mountains to find a slower pace of life. We relocated to Lewiston, California, a town of about nine hundred people way up in the Trinity Alps. Living in the wilderness was definitely slower than the traffic-packed city we had left behind. But it turned out that this only served to heighten my awareness of the rat race going on inside me.

As time passed, the fear intensified, affecting every aspect of our lives. I became claustrophobic to such an extent that I had to drive with the windows down in our car (even in the winter) so I would not panic. Although my personality is naturally outgoing, I became reclusive and never wanted to be around people. When friends came over to visit, I had Kathy get rid of them. I could not handle crowds, which eliminated shopping, restaurants, movies or doing anything in public. Although I continued to attend church, I sat in the back and got up to go outside several times during each service in order to reduce some of my crowd anxiety.

True to form, Kathy continued to take it all in stride. Though she was young, she somehow possessed great faith that we would get through it all. Looking back, I can see how the Lord had prepared her for this battle from the time she was young. Kathy's mother had severe epilepsy and suffered forty to fifty seizures a month. With her dad gone most of the time, Kathy was the one who stayed home from school to take care of her mom. Even as a young girl, she became the stabilizing force in the family. I thank God that she brought that same dynamic into our relationship.

Terrorist Attacks and a Prison Break

We opened a small automotive repair shop in Weaverville, California, a town about twenty miles from Lewiston. Although business was good, finances were tight. We got up early most mornings, put Jaime in a car seat, and went fishing for food in the river down the street from our house. Transitioning from two fairly significant incomes in the city to living on one meager salary out in the sticks was quite a culture shock. (The *Little House on the Prairie* lifestyle is definitely overrated!)

Two more years passed with no relief. Then, just when I thought it could not get any worse, I began to experience demonic visitations. Demons literally would come into our room at night and torment me. Lights went on and off, and pictures spontaneously fell off the wall! The phone rang every few minutes with people saying crazy things on the other end of the line. I am aware that many people do not believe in spirits, demons and angels, so this paragraph may be a little hard to swallow. But if you are reading this book and have had or are having similar experiences, I hope you believe in them now.

By the third year of this terrible storm, Kathy had had our second beautiful daughter, Shannon, but my life was becoming unbearable. The stress had caused my equilibrium to go crazy, making me nauseous all the time. Food ran right through me; I had diarrhea continually. I loved my family so much, but my inner torment was so intense that I did not want to live anymore. I was not going to kill myself; I just thought my family would be much better off if God took me home and Kathy found a "normal" husband. I cried out to God repeatedly, but He seemed distant . . . even uncaring. It seemed that the love I had known the first couple years in my walk with God had vanished, replaced by intense fear.

Then, early one cold winter morning, something startling happened. The four of us were still living in Lewiston, and as usual, I could not sleep. I got up about 3:00 A.M., wrapped a blanket around myself and went into the living room. I turned the stereo on low and lay down next to the speaker so I would not wake my family. Our radio reception was not good up in the mountains, but I thought I would try to find a late-night talk show to help get my mind off my condition.

Finally, I tuned in to some preacher. The static was so bad that I could only make out every third or fourth word of his message. Yet in the midst of the noise, I heard him say something that would forever change my life. He quoted Paul's exhortation to Timothy: "God has not given us a spirit of fear, but of power and of love and of a sound mind" (2 Timothy 1:7, NKJV). Then he went on to explain, "Fear is a spirit! Some of you are thinking you're going insane, but you're just listening to the spirit of insanity! Not all your thoughts are your own. Evil spirits talk to you by giving you their thoughts."

I was stunned! I had been taught that Christians could be mentally ill but could not be demonized. What I did not realize until that night was that I had been educated right out of my solution.

I turned off the radio and asked Jesus what I should do. Immediately I heard a Voice inside my spirit say, *You have been listening to the spirit of insanity and the spirit of fear. Tell them to leave you right now!*

Lying on my back on the living room floor, I said in a quiet but confident voice, "You spirit of fear and you spirit of insanity, get off me right now in Jesus' name!"

I could not see anything, but suddenly I felt something get up off my body. It physically felt like a lead blanket, the kind dentists use during X-rays, and it was being lifted off me. My shaking completely stopped, peace filled my soul and my mind was clear again. Joy overwhelmed my heart, and I laughed out loud for the first time in more than three years. A miracle had happened in my life, and I was eager to tell Kathy and the world about it.

Learning to Stay Free

I knew I had experienced something incredible that night, yet I did not fully understand that I had received a real deliverance.

The only deliverance ministry I had ever witnessed prior to this was something that looked similar to a person having a grand mal seizure, with Christians gathering around the poor soul and shouting at the demons to "come out!" The person often left those sessions more traumatized by the Christians than by the demons. I wanted no part of that kind of ministry. (I am certain there was healthy deliverance ministry going on in the Church, but I had not been exposed to it.)

What I experienced that night was not some kind of spiritual hype or psychosomatic occurrence. I was set free! I enjoyed complete freedom for more than a week. After three years of hell, being filled with peace was amazing. My joy returned, my appetite came back and all my physical symptoms disappeared. The demonic visitations left, and for the first time in years I slept through the night.

But soon I encountered the harsh reality that getting free and staying free were two very different things. One dark, cold night, I was driving home from work in my Jeep, winding through the forest on a narrow, unlit road that followed a wide creek. I was so excited about my newfound freedom that I shouted out loud; "I'm going to tell everyone about this—I'm going to help thousands of people get free!"

Just then a voice in my mind shouted back, *If you tell anyone about this, I'll kill you!*

Suddenly, all my symptoms returned. I had such a bad panic attack that I could not even drive. I pulled over into the ditch alongside the road. My heart was racing, and I was hyperventilating.

Then a quiet, yet powerful Voice asked me a question: *Does the devil hate you?* (I knew instinctively it was the Holy Spirit speaking to me this time.)

"*Yes!*" I responded.

Then why didn't he kill you when you got saved? the Voice pressed.

"*I don't know,*" I replied, still trying to gain my composure.

Because he can't! He has no power over you unless you give it to him, the Voice insisted.

Peace began to seep back into my soul, and the anxiety slowly lifted over the next few minutes.

I began to shout again, "I'm free! I'm free!"

That scene repeated itself many times over the next several years as I learned little by little how to stay free and keep my peace.

Free to Live in Peace

Almost three decades have passed since that fateful night when I had lain on the floor in our little house way up in the woods and had found freedom. Over these last thirty years, I have helped thousands of people get free, find solace and learn to live in peace.

Yet two years ago, I found myself in another intense personal battle that lasted almost seven months. I learned so much more in this struggle, and it helped me to understand another side of the war against fear, anxiety, oppression and depression. I feel as if I have a Ph.D. in the subject. Every time I share my experiences in a public setting, I am flooded with people telling me their stories and begging me for help.

I have read many Christian and secular books on the subjects of depression, oppression, fear, anxiety and panic. I have found some of them helpful. But frankly, many of these books are not only inaccurate, they are also destructive and actually lead to greater bondage.

I also have spoken to several mental health care professionals, as well as medical doctors, and found that few of them really understand the root causes of these symptoms. Part of the challenge is that most health care professionals, whether Christian or secular, view the spirit world as some kind of fairy tale perpetuated by uneducated and ignorant souls.

I have discovered as well that many Christian counselors who believe in the spirit world and minister to this dimension have very little insight into how intertwined our triune being is. We are composed of spirit, soul and body, and few counselors understand how much each dimension affects the others. These folks often think that every negative symptom in a person is rooted in the spirit. They are completely ineffective, therefore, in dealing with problems that have their origins in the other two-thirds of our being, the soul and the body.

Let me make it clear that there are Christian, Holy Spirit–filled counselors who *do* minister to each dimension of our triune being, but they seem few and far between. We certainly need more of these wise and insightful counselors who understand root causes and do not just treat symptomatic problems.

My most recent personal breakthrough finally inspired me to write a book on the subject myself. I actually started this book before my breakthrough, in the midst of the worst struggle of my life—which gives certain chapters a unique kind of battlefield perspective. This book is not meant to be the last word on mental or spiritual health. It is, however, written by someone who has firsthand experience in finding peace myself and helping multitudes of others do the same.

One of the pivotal truths I have learned through my journey is that we are *new creatures in Christ* (see 2 Corinthians 5:17), and therefore our battles in life are never with our old nature. Our flesh may be weak (see Mark 14:38), but it is no longer corrupt. The enemy works hard to convince us otherwise, so that instead of resisting him, we turn against ourselves. Self-sabotage is the common denominator in all forms of anxiety and depression, whether rooted in the body, soul or spirit. My main goal for this book is to help you gain insight into the ways we sabotage ourselves, give you wisdom for how to break free from these destructive patterns, and impart courage to you to face the real battles in life—battles you were made to win. You will learn how to live in joy, cultivate peace and protect yourself from the onslaughts of evil forces. You will find new freedom for yourself and learn new skills that will help you help others live a stress-free life.

May the Prince of Peace meet you in the pages of this book and lead you into complete wholeness—spirit, soul and body!

2

Are You Living in a Haunted House?

*N*estled in the tall pine trees on a narrow road that winds its way through the mountains is an aged log cabin. A steep cliff overshadows this old miner's bungalow, causing it rarely to see the light of day. An eerie sensation comes over you as you approach the well-worn front porch, straddle the rotten beams and reach for the rusted iron door handle. The door creaks with resistance as you force it into submission, finally revealing a gloomy room. A rotten, musty odor assails your senses, but you brave the threshold and make your way inside. Peering straight ahead, you sight a primitive river rock fireplace covered in black soot from years of use. To the right is an ancient handmade rocking chair, built from a tree harvested off that very mountain. The locals say that about a hundred years ago, the old miner who lived here was murdered in that very rocker. . . .

I hope this sounds like the beginning of a ghost story, be-cause it is—one I happened to experience for myself. That old cabin is up in the Trinity Alps, and a couple of my friends, desperate for a cheap place to live, once rented it—only to discover that it was haunted! I am not kidding you. The towns-folk warned them about the haunting, but they did not believe it. Then one dark, moonless night, the old miner appeared in their room, waking them from a dead sleep and scaring the daylights out of them. These visitations went on for months, until finally they decided to come talk to me about it.

We drove to the cabin, and I forged my way through the door with my two friends in tow. Fear, thick and tangible as a heavy fog, settled over my mind as I pressed forward into the dark room. All of a sudden, he appeared!

"Yikes!" I shuddered. The hair on the back of my head stood straight up. But what happened next forever changed my perspective on the spirit realm. I was immediately overcome by the thought, *This is not the old miner who has come back from the dead to terrify my friends, but a demon masquerad-ing as the deceased!*

That revelation released a new sense of authority in me. I boldly commanded the wicked demon to leave the building and never return. My friends looked on in complete horror as two kingdoms wrestled for dominance in that tiny room. But within a few minutes, the demon was gone and the old cabin was clean.

Kicking a Corpse

My ghost story affirms a powerful reality, the truth Paul taught the Ephesians: "For our struggle *is not* against flesh and blood, but against the rulers, against the powers, against the world forces of this darkness, against the spiritual forces of wickedness in the heavenly places" (Ephesians 6:12, emphasis added). Yet I have found that hordes of believers have fallen prey to the same demonic charade my friends experienced. They were told at baptism that their old selves had drowned in the sea of crucifixion. They can quote Galatians 2:20 and say they have been "crucified with Christ." They have all read the book of Romans, which tells them over thirty times that they are dead, they died, their old self was crucified, they should consider themselves dead . . . dead, dead, dead, dead, dead! (As I like to say, we are the original Grateful Dead.) And yet, they find that they keep being "haunted" by what appears to be their old man. Some of these folks end up spending their entire lives kicking a corpse, wrestling a carcass and otherwise wasting their energy on an enemy that has already died, while the real foe laughs sarcastically through the prison bars of their lives.

These Christians live on house arrest. Like spiritual archaeologists, they spend most of their time digging in the graveyard of their old lives, looking to unearth some hidden treasure of hope. But all they ever discover are the dry bones of discouragement, condemnation and fear.

How is it that so many believers are living in haunted houses? Simply put, they have not really learned how to live in the reality of the verses they can quote about having been crucified with Christ. They have not really understood the difference between who they used to be and who they have become. One of the reasons for this is that many of them misunderstand the way the New Testament uses the word *flesh*.

Practically all those who believe they are struggling with "the flesh" get that idea from the apostle Paul. He described his own battle with his sinful flesh in Romans 7:18–24:

> For I know that nothing good dwells in me, that is, in my flesh; for the willing is present in me, but the doing of the good is not. For the good that I want, I do not do, but I practice the very evil that I do not want. But if I am doing the very thing I do not want, I am no longer the one doing it, but sin which dwells in me. I find then the principle that evil is present in me, the one who wants to do good. For I joyfully concur with the law of God in the inner man, but I see a different law in the members of my body, waging war against the law of my mind and making me a prisoner of the law of sin which is in my members. Wretched man that I am! Who will set me free from the body of this death?

I know what you are thinking: *If the great apostle Paul, who wrote thirteen books of the New Testament, was in bondage to his sinful flesh, what are the chances that I won't struggle with sin?* This would be a good question if Paul were describing a struggle he had had while he was an apostle. But the truth is that in this passage, Paul is telling the story of his B.C. life, not his life in Christ. He uses present-tense language to emphasize the past-tense struggle he had as a Pharisee. He is describing what it was like to be a teacher of the Law of God without knowing Christ. The Law taught him right from wrong, but gave him no power to walk uprightly. And the more he learned about the Law of God, the guiltier he became (see Romans 5:20).

To really understand Paul's dissertation on what happened when he went from B.C. to A.D., we have to take a step back into the previous chapters of Romans so we can grasp the context of his comments in Romans 7.

What follows is a challenging and often misunderstood concept. Stay with me as I build a scriptural foundation here, and you will soon realize what life-changing truths Paul is presenting about sin and the believer. Let's look at a few verses in Romans 6:

> Are we to continue in sin so that grace may increase? May it never be! How shall we who died to sin still live in it? . . . knowing this, that our old self was crucified with Him, in order that our body of sin might be done away with, so that we would no longer be slaves to sin; for he who has died is freed from sin.
>
> Verses 1–2, 6–7

In these verses, Paul makes it clear that our old self "was crucified" with Christ (past tense), which resulted in our no longer being slaves to sin, because dead people do not sin! More, our "body of sin" (the same "body of this death" he talks about in chapter 7) has been done away with. In other words, that old corpse that people think they are kicking does not even exist anymore! When we believe it can come back, we empower a lie—which gives Satan, the father of lies, the opportunity to set up his haunted house in our lives. This is why Paul instructs us to align our beliefs with the truth: "Even so consider yourselves to be dead to sin, but alive to God in Christ Jesus. . . . For sin shall not be master over you, for you are not under law but under grace . . . having been freed from sin, you became slaves of righteousness" (Romans 6:11, 14, 18).

We are to consider ourselves dead to sin. That word *consider* in the Greek is an accounting term. It literally means that we are to take all the facts into account and come to this conclusion: *We are dead to sin.* It is like doing a math problem where we already know the answer. If we do the math and come up with a different answer, we need to go back and check our facts.

Remarriage Has Its Privileges

Now that we have seen how clear Paul was about our being dead to sin, let's examine Paul's opening statements in Romans 7, right before he talks about struggling with his flesh, to see if we can gain some deeper insight into his exhortation:

> Or do you not know, brethren (for I am speaking to those who know the law), that the law has jurisdiction over a person as long as he lives? For the married woman is bound by law to her husband while he is living; but if her husband dies, she is released from the law concerning the husband. So then, if while her husband is living she is joined to another man, she shall be called an adulteress; but if her husband dies, she is free from the law, so that she is not an adulteress though she is joined to another man. Therefore, my brethren, you also were made to die to the Law through the body of Christ, so that you might be joined to another, to Him who was raised from the dead, in order that we might bear fruit for God. For while we were in the flesh, the sinful passions, which were aroused by the Law, were at work in the members of our body to bear fruit for death. But now we have been released from the Law, having died to that by which we were bound, so that we serve in newness of the Spirit and not in oldness of the letter.
>
> Romans 7:1–6

Paul describes our journey out of the bondage of sin by using the analogy of marriage. Marriage, like the Law, is a covenant only broken by death. If a woman divorces her husband and then marries someone else, the Law says she is an adulteress. But if her first husband dies and then she remarries, she is not an adulteress because her husband's death dissolved the bond between them.

How does Paul's analogy apply to us? The Law—the Old Covenant—was our first husband. But in our case, we were the ones who died. When Christ died on the cross, we died with Him and our covenant with the Law ended. Then, when Christ rose again, we rose with Him and were *joined* (married) to Him in the New Covenant. Christ, who rescued us from the clutches of the Law, also became our new husband! And in this new marriage, we are no longer bound under the demands of the old marriage.

I heard a great story many years ago that demonstrates the difference between being married to our first husband, Mr. Law, and being married to Mr. Grace, Jesus Christ. The account is supposedly a true story, though I have never been able to confirm it. A beautiful young woman married her childhood sweetheart. Immediately after the wedding, her husband revealed himself as an angry, mean tyrant. Sitting on the bed on their honeymoon night, he handed her a list of duties and responsibilities he *demanded* that she fulfill as his wife. She spent the next ten years trying to comply with all his rules, but she never could measure up. Then one day, her husband dropped dead from a heart attack.

A few years later, this wonderful woman married again. This time, she married a real prince! He loved her and lavished her with affection. They had an amazing marriage.

Many years passed, and one day as she was cleaning out her old hope chest, she ran across the list her first husband had given her on their honeymoon. As she reviewed his demands, anxiety began to fill her heart. Then something remarkable happened. She suddenly realized that all the demands she could never fulfill when she was married to the mean husband had become the things she did naturally for years out of passion for her prince!

This is precisely what Paul is saying in Romans 7. He is recounting the terrible sense of bondage he experienced when he lived under a set of rules but never knew his lover. He does so to help us understand the amazing contrast between the old marriage and the new marriage.

A New Spirit, Mind and Body

Paul begins Romans 8 by showing us how completely different we are now that we have been "joined to another man." Our triune being—body, soul and spirit—has undergone a radical transformation:

> For the law of the Spirit of life in Christ Jesus has set you free from the law of sin and of death. For what the Law could not do, weak as it was through the flesh, God did: sending His own Son in the likeness of sinful flesh and as an offering for sin, He condemned sin in the flesh. . . . For those who are according to the flesh set their minds on the things of the flesh, but those who are according to the Spirit, the things of the Spirit. For the mind set on the flesh is death, but the mind set on the Spirit is life and peace, because the mind set on the flesh is hostile toward God; for it does not subject itself to the law of God, for it is not even able to do so, and

those who are in the flesh cannot please God. However, you are not in the flesh but in the Spirit, if indeed the Spirit of God dwells in you. But if anyone does not have the Spirit of Christ, he does not belong to Him. . . . He who raised Christ Jesus from the dead will also give life to your mortal bodies through His Spirit who dwells in you. . . . For all who are being led by the Spirit of God, these are sons of God. For you have not received a spirit of slavery leading to fear again, but you have received a spirit of adoption as sons by which we cry out, "Abba! Father!"

Romans 8:2–3, 5–9, 11, 14–15

This passage shows us the state of our spirit, soul and body before Christ, as well as our state in Christ. When we were married to the Law, our spirits were dead, separated from God through sin. This spiritual death left our minds (souls) under the control of the sinful demands and passions of our corrupt bodies. But Christ ended our separation from God by taking the condemnation for sin on Himself, allowing our spirits to be joined to His Spirit and come alive. This in turn allowed our minds to be "set" on His Spirit, which ended the war between the mind and the body and brought us life and peace. Finally, our bodies, which had been "sinful flesh," shared in Christ's death. That killed the disease of sin, and in His resurrection, He gave life to our mortal bodies. Our bodies have gone from evil castles, housing a sinful nature that "cannot please God," to holy temples in which the Holy Spirit "dwells."

God left no part of us unchanged when He married us to His Son. This is why in Paul's second letter to the Corinthians, he says that we are a "new creation"—not just a new spirit, but an entirely new being (2 Corinthians 5:17, NKJV). Our very nature has been completely transformed. We have been changed from those who were hostile toward God into saints who love Jesus with their entire being—spirit, soul and *body*!

But wait, you might think, *didn't Paul just say that the flesh was hostile toward God?* Look again. He said, "the mind set on the flesh is hostile toward God." What does this mean? It will become clearer if you study how the New Testament uses the Greek word *sarx,* which is usually translated "flesh." You will find that the word itself does not denote something negative or positive—both the old nature and the new creation are called "the flesh" (*sarx*) in different contexts. This tells us that our physical body is not the source of good or evil. Our flesh is governed by our spirit and our soul. In particular, our soul is the operating system of the body, the mediator between the spiritual and the physical. The "mind set on the flesh" is a description of the soul that is disconnected from the Holy Spirit and is running a "program" built on lies and false spiritual power, like lust and fear. In his letter to the Galatians, Paul described the behavior this mindset produces: "Now the deeds of the flesh are evident, which are: immorality, impurity, sensuality, idolatry, sorcery, enmities, strife, jealousy, outbursts of anger, disputes, dissensions, factions, envying, drunkenness, carousing, and things like these" (Galatians 5:19–21).

But again, when our spirits were made alive in Christ, our souls were set free of the tyranny of this mindset. We now have the freedom and responsibility to "set our minds" on the things of the Spirit. When our minds are set on the Spirit, we no longer are controlled by our physical passions. Instead, we have the power to direct our bodies according to their true spiritual value and purpose.

First, Paul teaches us that we are to nourish and cherish our flesh: "For no one ever hated his own flesh, but nourishes and cherishes it, just as Christ also does the church, because we are members of His body" (Ephesians 5:29–30). The Greek word for *cherish* here is *thalpo*, the same Greek word that is translated "tenderly cares" in 1 Thessalonians 2:7: "We proved to be gentle among you, as a nursing mother tenderly cares for her own children." If the flesh of our new man were opposed to God, the Bible certainly would not teach us to take care of it the way a mother tenderly nurses her child.

Second, Paul says in Romans 6:13 to present "your members as instruments of righteousness to God," and in Romans 12:1 to present "your bodies a living and holy sacrifice, acceptable to God." If you have read the Old Testament, you know that the only things that could be used as "instruments" or "sacrifices" for the worship of God were things that had been purified and cleansed. It would have been impossible for the Jews in Rome, to whom Paul wrote this letter, to miss the implication of these verses: Our bodies are clean and pure in Christ.

Self-Deception

Now let's get practical. Perhaps you are asking yourself, *If we really are new creations and no longer battle with the flesh, then how is it that believers still sin? Doesn't this mean we still have a sin nature?*

Let me ask you this: Did Adam and Eve have a sin nature when they fell? The answer is no. Adam and Eve proved that you do not need a sin nature to sin. After God created Adam, both male and female, He looked out at *all* He made and said it was "very good" (Genesis 1:31). If Adam and Eve had possessed a sin nature, God could not have called them "very good."

This proves that all you need to sin is a free will and the capacity to believe a lie. All believers possess these qualities—that is why the apostle John taught us not to deceive ourselves about who we were before we were cleansed from sin and who we are after we are cleansed:

> If we say that we have no sin, we are deceiving ourselves and the truth is not in us. If we confess our sins, He is faithful and righteous to forgive us our sins and to cleanse us from all unrighteousness. . . . My little children, *I am writing these things to you so that you may not sin. And if anyone sins, we have an Advocate with the Father, Jesus Christ the righteous.*
>
> 1 John 1:8–9; 2:1, emphasis added

John makes it clear that all of us come to Christ as people who "have sin"—that is, who are prone to sin. After all, God only saves sinners. No matter how nice, caring, generous or friendly people are, they are still inherently prone to wrongdoing if they do not know Jesus. Thus, the first way we can deceive ourselves is by saying we have no sin that needs to be forgiven.

But the goal of John's letter is that we would *not* sin, which is only possible if the cleansing we receive from Christ removed our old proneness to sin. This is what the new creation experience of baptism did to us. Our old nature drowned, and we came up from the water with a new spirit, a spirit that cries, "Abba, Father!" In the core of our beings, we are now wonderful people who inherently love and long for our heavenly Father, just as Christ does. There is no evil intrinsically present in us. We have heaven's heart.

In fact, God has done so much to set us up for a holy life that *if* (not when) we sin, we actually need an advocate to help plead our case. Thus, after we have confessed our sins, the second way we can deceive ourselves is by saying that we know God while continuing to *practice* sin. And one of the best ways to do this is to embrace the belief that we are still sinners by nature. If we believe we are sinners, we will continue to sin.

This is why John teaches us to believe that we will not sin as we learn to abide in Christ. He writes, "No one who abides in Him sins; no one who sins has seen Him or knows Him. . . . No one who is born of God practices sin, because His seed abides in him; and he cannot sin, because he is born of God" (1 John 3:6, 9).

Wow! These are strong words: *"No one who is born of God practices sin"!* These passages really drive home the point I am making. Those of us who know God are *not* in a war with our flesh. We are no longer sinners. But we do have a devious, evil enemy who is a sinner. He is endlessly accusing the Body of having his own wicked nature. He is trying to get us to believe him, to forget who we really are and to disqualify ourselves from our divine destiny of putting him under our feet.

Let me be clear that I am not saying we will never *choose* to sin or never need to repent once we are born again. As I said, all it takes to sin is a free will and the capacity to believe the lies of the enemy—and believers possess both. We may indeed choose to sin, and consequently we will need to repent. What I am saying is that we do not naturally sin because we no longer have a *sin nature* that is married to the Law. Our old nature has been crucified with Christ; we are new creations married to Christ in the New Covenant.

In opposition to this powerful truth, a deceptive theology keeps circulating through the Church—a doctrine that basically says it is still our nature to sin after we have been born again. I am convinced this is a doctrine of demons. The devil wants to convince us that sin, wickedness, addictions and every other form of bondage are rooted in our nature. That way, he can torment us and then blame it on our old man. But in the parable of the lost sheep, Jesus said, "There will be more joy in heaven over one sinner who repents than over ninety-nine righteous persons who need no repentance" (Luke 15:7). This parable demonstrates the common state of most people in the Kingdom—according to Jesus, ninety-nine out of a hundred people in God need *no repentance*! The normal Christian life is not supposed to be an exhausting wrestling match with a dead man, but is an abundant, joy-filled life with God, salted with an occasional season of strong resistance from our archenemy.

Misery Loves Company

This deceptive perception that born-again believers are still sinners by nature raised its ugly head awhile back when I was teaching a group about the divine nature of born-again people. I was telling the class that we are no longer sinners, but instead have become saints through the power of the cross.

To illustrate my point, I said, "There is a river that flows through our souls, and it runs toward the throne. If we don't paddle, we will end up at God's house! You have to make an effort to sin because it is no longer your nature."

A tall young man in the middle of the room just could not take it any longer. He abruptly stood to his feet and with all the passion he could muster shouted out, "Have you ever had a day go by that you didn't sin?"

"Yes, of course I have," I shot back.

"How about a week?" he pressed, staring me right in the eyes with a stern look.

"Sure," I continued, smiling at him. "In fact, I have gone several weeks in a row without sinning."

He flopped down in his seat, looking completely defeated. It seemed strange to me that he did not find my comments encouraging. After all, I was not saying that I was perfect or had accomplished anything wonderful by my own strength or self-discipline. I know well that the best efforts of man only lead to the prison of self-righteousness. I was simply attesting to the Holy Spirit's work in my life. It is the Holy Spirit's responsibility to lead us into all truth and perfect us from the inside out.

In the previous chapter, I shared my personal story of demonic bondage and torment. One of the main reasons my battle lasted so long was that I was fighting the wrong enemy. Misguided teaching had convinced me that my tormenting thoughts, night terrors and intense fear were the manifestations of the war we all have with our old man. Nobody ever told me that this terrifying season was actually a war with demonic spirits whose goal was to steal, kill and destroy my life. Through the years since then, I have learned that although warfare is a normal part of a believer's life in certain seasons, there are several ways that we actually empower evil spirits to torture us. In the next chapter, we will uncover some of the deceptive traps Christians often fall into that imprison their souls and captivate their hearts.

3

Rules of Engagement

Spiritual conflicts most often occur when we advance into new territory currently inhabited by evil spirits. Just as enemies fought Joshua in the Promised Land and Nehemiah as he rebuilt the walls of Jerusalem, so will our enemy fight us when we begin to take the spiritual terrain God has promised to us. Most Christians, however, are completely unaware that the resistance they encounter as they step into God's promises is actually part of a spirit war. They retreat at the first sign of conflict because they fail to recognize the true source of the battle or the way in which war is waged in the invisible realm.

One of the most common ways demonic spirits attack is by giving us thoughts that the Bible describes as flaming arrows (see Ephesians 6:16). Because these thoughts are actually manifestations of evil spirits and not just bad ideas, they are compelling—in other words, there is unction to do the act that we are contemplating, even though these ideas are contrary to our new nature. Then these same spirits accuse us of originating these thoughts and impulses. If we believe their accusations, we lose confidence in our identity and digress into emotions like depression, anxiety and self-hatred.

The enemy and his cohorts also attack our imaginations by inspiring terrible visions or pictures that wrestle against our minds and can be deeply troubling, especially if we do not understand the source of these assaults. The same unction that accompanies false thoughts usually accompanies these false visions.

Some people experience warfare without a thought or picture in their minds, but with awful "feelings," false impulses or unctions that rage against their souls. But no matter what manifestations spiritual warfare takes on, the most important fact to remember is that these are symptoms of the enemy's devious plot to steal our inheritance, kill our offspring and destroy our very lives.

Demonic Survey

Recently I began to wonder how many people were actually aware of the war taking place in their souls and affecting their minds. I decided to do my own "demonic attack survey" to find out. At the conferences I spoke at around the world, I posed this simple question: "How many of you have been driving down the road, minding your own business, when out of the blue you have the thought that you should crash your car into something and kill yourself, followed by an unction so intense that you feel as though you have to hold onto the steering wheel with both hands just so you don't do something stupid? Please raise your hand if this has happened to you."

The results stunned me. I probably surveyed more than ten thousand people this past year, and two-thirds of them acknowledged having this exact experience. It is comforting for people who respond yes to look around the room and observe the number and quality of the other people with their hands raised. Most people attesting to this experience are stable saints with great reputations. Many people have come up to me after these meetings to share how reassuring it is to know they are not crazy.

Paul explains this spirit war strategy in 2 Corinthians 10:3–5, where he says that the enemy attacks us with *thoughts, speculations* and *lofty things*. The enemy tries to get us to entertain and agree with these thoughts. If we do, brick by brick they become fortresses, evil castles of destructive ideas that imprison our souls, leaving us longing for a prince to rescue us from the clutches of our wicked captor.

The fact that Paul describes our dealing with these things as "the destruction of fortresses" (verse 4) rather than simply as changing our thoughts suggests that although thoughts, speculations and lofty things are not tangible in this realm, they are in the spirit world. They are demonically inspired realities that the enemy seeks to fulfill through our cooperation.

Thoughts are often random ideas like the one I shared in my car crash example, while *speculations* and *lofty things* are systems of thought that are more strategically destructive in their focus. *Speculations* are often characterized by what-if questions, which if left unchecked, can plague our souls. "What if I have cancer?" "What if my wife is late getting home because she's having an affair?" "What if my son or daughter is taking drugs?" "What if my daughter gets pregnant on a date?" Notice that none of these what-ifs suggest good things to us. Speculations prey upon our fears, seeking open doors in our lives through which they can lead us into bondage.

Lofty things are philosophies that make us feel the devil is big and powerful and God is small and powerless in our lives. Expressions like "Well, I guess all we can do now is pray" are the fruit of a "lofty things" mentality. When we are under this spirit's influence, our circumstances easily overwhelm us. We feel like little children in a grown-up world.

Paul also reminded us that these epic battles that rage against our minds are not due to human nature. We are not warring against flesh and blood, but against demonic forces of evil. Paul established this truth in Ephesians 6:12 when he said, "Our struggle is not against flesh and blood, but against the rulers, against the powers, against the world forces of this darkness, against the spiritual forces of wickedness in the heavenly places." In the previous chapter, we looked at this verse in light of our new nature. But I want to reiterate that because we have this new nature, we can be sure that these thoughts do not originate in our minds—they are sponsored advertisements from the dark side. One of the most important keys to winning these battles is simply to recognize that these thoughts are not our own and to reject all ownership of them. As Paul told the Philippians, when we refuse to be impressed, alarmed or concerned by these thoughts, it is a sign of destruction for our opponents and of victory for us (see Philippians 1:28).

The Demon with Glowing Eyes

Many years ago, I learned firsthand how to apply Philippians 1:28 when terrible dreams began to torment me. I would often wake up in a panic at seeing two large, glowing red eyes watching me from the foot of my bed. (I know this sounds like a scene from a horror movie, but it is true.) This went on for months. I tried everything I could think of to get it to stop. I rebuked the thing in Jesus' name. I read Scriptures to it for hours. I worshiped God while it watched—nothing seemed to faze it. Then one day the Lord gave me the Philippians principle: *In no way be alarmed by your opponents, which is a sign of destruction for them, but of salvation for you.* He called this *"the power of ignore."*

That very night the demon returned. I woke up to the same scenario, but this time I was ready. With my heart pounding out of my chest, I looked up at that demon with red, glowing eyes and said in a calm voice, "Oh, it's just you again." And then I rolled over and went to sleep. It never came back after that night. I realized that when the evil spirit lost the ability to scare me, it no longer had power over me.

Through these battles, I have learned several principles that are important to remember in these times. First, evil spirits have no power over Christians (even though it feels as if they do) *unless* we give it to them. We have power over them! Second, these battles come in waves, and they will not last forever. And third, we probably did nothing wrong to cause the battles. As a matter of fact, we are usually in a battle because we are doing something right.

Engaging in Conflict

I want to identify some "rules of engagement" I have drawn from the epic story of Nehemiah that will help us recognize and defeat these demonic impulses and attacks. Understanding the rules of engagement is paramount if we are to win these battles instead of becoming POWs in a demonic prison camp. The book of Nehemiah gives us several great insights into these rules.

Nehemiah was a Jewish cupbearer to a king in a foreign country. Hanani, Nehemiah's brother, came to visit him and told him about how things were going in Jerusalem (see Nehemiah 1:2–11). Years before, Ezra the priest had led a group of Israelites in rebuilding Solomon's Temple, which had been destroyed in the war with the Babylonians. But though they had managed to rebuild the Temple, the Israelites had found it impossible, despite years of rigorous effort, to rebuild the walls and set up the gates around Jerusalem. These walls and gates were necessary to ensure the protection of the people and define the boundaries of their inheritance.

When Nehemiah heard about Jerusalem's decrepit condition, he became distraught and asked the king for a leave of absence so he could assess the situation and help with the city's restoration. The king gave him more than a leave of absence; he commissioned Nehemiah to rebuild the walls. He also sent help and provision, and he extended the favor he had with neighboring nations by asking them to assist Nehemiah in procuring building materials necessary to complete the job (see Nehemiah 2:1–9).

The name Nehemiah means "comforter," and his work of rebuilding the walls of Jerusalem is a beautiful picture of how the Comforter, the Holy Spirit, works to restore the boundaries in our lives and bring us to perfection (see Hebrews 7:11; 11:40; 12:23; James 3:2; 1 Peter 5:10). Like the city of Jerusalem in the days of Ezra, when we receive Jesus as our Lord, the first thing God does is rebuild His temple within us. But our "walls and gates" are still in need of repair. Isaiah said, "You will call your walls salvation, and your gates praise" (Isaiah 60:18). In the New Testament, the Greek word for salvation, *sozo*, refers not only to spiritual resurrection, but also to the total restoration of our bodies and souls. The Holy Spirit rebuilds our "walls of salvation" by correcting our old, broken patterns of thinking and establishing new strongholds of truth that bring health and strength to every dimension of our beings. As the Holy Spirit restores us, He trains our wills to choose thoughts, values and behaviors that bring Him praise.

"Gates" represent access points in our hearts that hinge on guarded choices we make. When evil elements of deception have infected many of our pivotal choices, our gates become rusty doors of indifference unaccustomed to closing to protect us from the cold wind of worldly thinking. As long as we remain apathetic, lethargic and passive, the demonic spirits behind our infected choices stay concealed and go unnoticed because the enemy has free access to our heart and minds. It is only when we shake off complacency and close the gates of our minds to demonic thinking that all hell seems to break loose. The enemy wars against us when we proactively embrace our destiny by cutting him off at the gates.

Let's take a peek behind the veil of time and see if we can catch a glimpse into the nature of these invisible conflicts that war over the walls and gates of our souls. We will spy out the enemy's strategies in Nehemiah's historic exploits to rebuild Jerusalem's walls. Here is Nehemiah's own account of how he managed to instigate a conflict with the enemy when he determined to pursue his destiny and claim his people's inheritance:

I came to the governors of the provinces beyond the River and gave them the king's letters. Now the king had sent with me officers of the army and horsemen. When Sanballat the Horonite and Tobiah the Ammonite official heard about it, it was very displeasing to them that someone had come to seek the welfare of the sons of Israel.

Nehemiah 2:9–10

The devil hates to see restoration in any area of our lives or in the lives of others. Again, the warfare he wages against us is most often a sign that we have truly embraced the passionate pursuit of our Promised Land. I am reminded of this principle year after year as hundreds of students attend Bethel School of Supernatural Ministry. I recognize a common theme with most of our students as I listen to their personal stories. The conversation goes something like this: "Before I came to school, everything in my life was great. I had peace, my connection with God was good and my thoughts weren't crazy! But ever since I've started school, things have been so hard. I'm not sure what I'm doing wrong, but I just feel as if I'm weaker than I've ever been before. . . ."

What most of our students fail to recognize is that the battle they are facing is not a sign from God that they have chosen the wrong path, but rather an indication that they have begun the process of restoring the walls and gates of their lives.

Strategic Restoration

When Nehemiah arrived in Jerusalem, the first thing he did was survey the walls and assess the problem. Likewise, the work of the Holy Spirit puts us in touch with our brokenness. In the name of "faith," however, many people refuse to face their problems head-on. They often tell others that they are believing God for a miracle and are therefore focusing on His Word, not on their troubles. Of course, this is a legitimate spiritual strategy that we will address later on in the book. But anytime we cannot look at our challenges without getting discouraged, we are living in denial, not faith. For example, if you do not balance your checkbook because you "believe" God takes care of your finances, you will probably learn this famous adage the hard way: "When your outgo exceeds your income, your upkeep will be your downfall." Denial is the fruit of fear, not the root of faith. True faith can evaluate the circumstances without growing hopeless because it sees the world through God's eyes.

Nehemiah was a realist. He knew he could not develop a strategy for rebuilding the walls and gates until he had accurately assessed the damages. Let's take a look at the way Nehemiah carried out this assessment:

> I came to Jerusalem and was there three days. And I arose in the night, I and a few men with me. I did not tell anyone what my God was putting into my mind to do for Jerusalem and there was no animal with me except the animal on which I was riding. So I went out at night by the Valley Gate in the direction of the Dragon's Well and on to the Refuse Gate, inspecting the walls of Jerusalem which were broken down and its gates which were consumed by fire. Then I passed on to the Fountain Gate and the King's Pool, but there was no place for my mount to pass. So I went up at night by the ravine and inspected the wall. Then I entered the Valley Gate again and returned. The officials did not know where I had

gone or what I had done; nor had I as yet told the Jews, the priests, the nobles, the officials or the rest who did the work.

Nehemiah 2:11–16

Nehemiah *"arose in the night"* and *"didn't tell anyone"* what God put in his heart to do for Jerusalem. This is a prophetic statement about how the Holy Spirit works in our lives to restore and perfect us. I have found that it is in the dark times (night) of our lives that the Lord begins to "arise" and shine His spotlight on our brokenness in order to make us whole. But in these night seasons when He is doing the most work in our lives, we are often completely unaware of it, or we think it is the devil. We must discern the difference between the Holy Spirit's searchlight, which assesses the damage done to our walls in order to rebuild us, and the accusations of evil spirits, which point out our weaknesses but have no redemptive value whatsoever.

Look at the contrast between Nehemiah's view of the situation and that of Israel's enemies, who focused on the weaknesses they perceived. Nehemiah's perspective was this:

Then I said to them, "You see *the bad situation we are in, that Jerusalem is desolate and its gates burned by fire.* Come, let us rebuild the wall of Jerusalem so that we will no longer be a reproach." I told them how the hand of my God had been favorable to me and also about the king's words which he had spoken to me. Then they said, "Let us arise and build." So they put their hands to the good work.

Nehemiah 2:17–18, emphasis added

Israel's enemies saw this:

Now it came about that when Sanballat heard that we were rebuilding the wall, he became furious and very angry and mocked the Jews. He spoke in the presence of his brothers and the wealthy men of Samaria and said, *"What are these feeble Jews doing? Are they going to restore it for themselves? Can they offer sacrifices? Can they finish in a day? Can they revive the stones from the dusty rubble even the burned ones?"* Now Tobiah the Ammonite was near him and he said, *"Even what they are building—if a fox should jump on it, he would break their stone wall down!"*

Nehemiah 4:1–3, emphasis added

Nehemiah, like the Holy Spirit in our lives, had an honest perspective on the condition of the walls and gates. He did not candy-coat it or play it down; neither did he try to make the people feel guilty for their condition. Instead he said, "You see the bad situation *we* are in." Nehemiah stated the truth about the problem and then took an equal share in its ownership. Likewise, when the Holy Spirit confronts our brokenness, He says, "Come now, and let us reason together" (Isaiah 1:18). In other words, "Let's figure this thing out together and fix it." But until we take equal ownership of our issues, He cannot help us solve them. As long as we insist that a terrible situation is not our fault or we blame our junk on someone else, our walls stay broken. We remain Pharisees who cross the street to avoid pain (see Luke 10:29–32) or critics who distance ourselves by criticizing anyone who is trying to help us. It is only as we take responsibility for a problem that we begin to be part of the solution.

In Nehemiah's story, Sanballat and Tobiah are like our archenemy the devil and his demons. They have no interest in seeing our walls restored. They only want to remind us of our weaknesses, with the intention of destroying us. If they cannot find a real problem in our lives, they will make some up. The apostle John described the devil as "the accuser of our brethren . . . who accuses them before our God day and night" (Revelation 12:10). The devil has made a career out of assaulting us. He is an equal opportunity destroyer. He does not care about our track record. He will employ his accusations against us no matter who we are.

Lying Speculations

Let's peer back in time at that last passage again to see what else we can glean from Nehemiah's diary. Here, the enemies are not employing any subtle tactics like temptation; they are resorting to a full-on accusatory attack. They use the same five accusations that our enemy most commonly levels at us as believers!

1. *"What are these feeble Jews doing?"* First, the devil attacks our personhood.
2. *"Are they going to restore it for themselves?"* Next, the accuser questions our motives.
3. *"Can they offer sacrifices?"* Then he tries to get us to doubt our relationship with God.
4. *"Can they finish it in a day? Can they revive the stones from the dusty rubble?"* The enemy tries to convince us that we do not have the ability to accomplish the mission.
5. *"Even what they are doing, if a fox should jump on it, it will fall down."* Finally, he attacks the quality of our work.

The schemes, plots and plans of the enemy have not changed in thousands of years. You would think by now we would recognize his devices and circumvent his conquests. But I am stunned by how often I see people gunned down at the same crime scene with the same lying speculations the devil has used for generations, even though the scene is clearly marked with the CAUTION tape of hundreds of Scriptures.

Here are a few keys to overcoming these common assaults. First, it is imperative that we never talk to the devil without our attorney present. Jesus is our advocate (see 1 John 2:1), and we should by no means negotiate with a terrorist! We should always let the Lord take up our case.

Observe how the Lord dealt with Satan when he brought charges against Joshua the high priest. I am sure Joshua was experiencing one of those hard seasons in his life where the devil was reminding him day and night of his failures, shortcomings and sins:

> Then he showed me Joshua the high priest standing before the angel of the LORD, and Satan standing at his right hand to accuse him. The LORD said to Satan, "The LORD rebuke you, Satan! Indeed, the LORD who has chosen Jerusalem rebuke you! Is this not a brand plucked from the fire?" Now Joshua was clothed with filthy garments and standing before the angel. He spoke and said to those who were standing before him, saying, "Remove the filthy garments from him." Again he said to him, "See, I have taken your iniquity away from you and will clothe you with festal robes."
>
> Zechariah 3:1–4

The Lord's work in our lives is an open rebuke to the powers of darkness. When evil princes mess with us, they trespass into dangerous territory. We are made righteous by God's works and not our own, and the truth of His grace overrides the devil's facts and fallacies.

Jesus has invited us to "draw near with confidence to the throne of grace, so that we may receive mercy and find grace to help in time of need" (Hebrews 4:16). When terrorist spirits are hunting us down, we can run into the palace, jump up on the throne and be seated with Christ. In fact, if things get too bad, we can play dead and hide in Christ (see Colossians 3:3). When my soul is under siege, I often have this vision of myself sitting on this huge throne with Jesus. The chair is so high that He has to help me up onto His lap. With my legs dangling several feet from the floor, I whisper in His ear, sharing with Him how someone is stalking me and will not leave me alone. The enemy seems terrified as he peers through the window of the palace and sees me whispering to the Lord. He suddenly flees the premises as the Lord gives the order to punish him for harassing me.

War—A Family Affair

Let's pick up on Nehemiah's story again:

> When the Jews who lived near them came and told us ten times, "They will come up against us from every place where you may turn," then I stationed men in the lowest parts of the space behind the wall, the exposed places, and I stationed the people in families with their swords, spears and bows. When I saw their fear, I rose and spoke to the nobles, the officials and the rest of the people: "Do not be afraid of them; remember the Lord who is great and awesome, and

fight for your brothers, your sons, your daughters, your wives and your houses."

Nehemiah 4:12–14

I love the fact that Nehemiah made war a family affair, stationing relatives in the wall's exposed places. This story reminds me of a situation we faced with our youngest son, Jason. When he was fifteen, he found himself in a terrible battle with pornography. A couple of months into his struggle, he told Kathy and me about his bondage and his unsuccessful fight to free himself. We advised him to tell the rest of the family and let us protect the broken-down places in the walls of his life until he had fortified his heart again. He agreed to let us join him in the battle.

The fight lasted for nearly nine months. Jason slipped several times back into the cesspool of porn. We all prayed for him daily and reminded him often of who he was called to be. We held him accountable for his thoughts, attitudes and behavior on a regular basis and stayed close to him during extra-hard days. The intense warfare finally lifted, and we celebrated together. We never condemned or accused him. We just kept letting him know that he was way too awesome to act like that. He was called to be a noble man, not some tramp who sexualizes the daughters of God.

Jason is 31 at the writing of this book and has never fallen into pornography again. The other day I heard him say, "I've often found myself in circumstances that were too big for me. But I've never faced anything in life that was too big for my family."

Nehemiah exhorted the Jews to fight for "your brothers, your sons, your daughters and your wives." It is important

for us to understand that our personal victories have corporate ramifications. No one ever fails alone! But when we
win freedom in our own lives, we are empowered to give it
to others as an inheritance.

Fear—Nuclear Arsenal of Demonic Powers

Nehemiah found that *fear* was the primary detractor of God's
work being accomplished in the people's lives. Fear is faith in
the wrong god. When we put our faith in Jesus, we experience the fruit of the Holy Spirit: "love, joy, peace, patience,
kindness, goodness, faithfulness, gentleness, self-control"
(Galatians 5:22–23). But when we listen to the wrong spirit,
poisoned produce begins to grow on the thornbush of anxiety,
reaping a harvest of destruction.

Fear is the most socially accepted sin in the Church. Fear
is a serial killer, the prime suspect in the death of more
people on the planet than all other diseases combined.
Fear in every form has been linked to heart disease, cancer, autoimmune disorders, mental illness and many other
sicknesses. Fear is the welcome mat to demonic activity in
our lives. The prophet Isaiah wrote, "You will be far from
oppression, for you will not fear" (Isaiah 54:14). When we
reject fear, we live in peace. But if we allow fear to creep
into our lives, we soon find ourselves oppressed, tormented
and tortured.

It is important for us to understand how critically God
views fear. For example, King David committed adultery with
Bathsheba and murdered her husband, Uriah, yet God did
not remove him from the throne (see 2 Samuel 11:1–27). On
the other hand, because King Saul feared the people whom

God had called him to lead, he disobeyed the Lord, and the Lord tore the kingship from him and gave it to David (see 1 Samuel 15:24–26).

Certainly, adultery and murder are terrible evils that qualify as social ills. I am not discounting that; I am simply trying to emphasize how the destructive nature of fear often goes completely unnoticed by society, though all the while it is quietly stealing our destiny, killing our bodies and destroying our cities.

Nehemiah's cure for his people's anxiety was simply to "remember the Lord who is great and awesome" (Nehemiah 4:14). Fear *dismembers* and *disfigures* our perspective of God, making Him seem a powerless pawn controlled by our circumstances. But when we *re-member* the Lord and *re-count* His works, we begin to *re-form* our vision of His greatness in our hearts. As we meditate on His greatness, confidence begins to sprout in the soil of our faith, and soon fear's fantasy is unmasked, flogged and sent fleeing.

The Weapon of Significance

Nehemiah's incredible success was dependent on his learning to master fear and his refusal to let go of his destiny. He and the Israelites persevered, and even though they literally had to build with a tool in one hand and a weapon in the other, they managed to finish their project in fewer than two months! This project was so threatening that their enemies relentlessly tried to stop it, to the bitter end. When Sanballat and his evil band of thugs saw that they could not stop the people, they decided to destroy Nehemiah personally by trying to distract him:

Now when it was reported to Sanballat, Tobiah, to Geshem the Arab and to the rest of our enemies that I had rebuilt the wall, and that no breach remained in it, although at that time I had not set up the doors in the gates, then Sanballat and Geshem sent a message to me, saying, "Come, let us meet together at Chephirim in the plain of Ono." But they were planning to harm me. So I sent messengers to them, saying, "I am doing a great work and I cannot come down. Why should the work stop while I leave it and come down to you?" They sent messages to me four times in this manner, and I answered them in the same way.

Nehemiah 6:1–4

Sanballat invited Nehemiah to meet him in the plain of Ono. *Ono* means "strength"—it is the stronghold of destruction for us. If you go down to that kind of plain, you will figure out why they named it Oh-No! When we are under assault, we must stay on high ground. We never want to battle our enemy at the place of *his* strength, where he has a strategic advantage to set up an ambush against us. The only exception to this rule of engagement is when the Holy Spirit leads us into the wilderness—then He will protect us. But we do not want to be one of those sheep who goes astray and finds itself alone, surrounded by wolves.

Nehemiah stayed out of the valley of Ono by reminding himself that he was called to greatness. He reminded his accusers of the same with this bold statement: "I am doing a great work and I cannot come down." We are all called to greatness, but greatness in a specific way for a specific assignment. It is so important that we know ourselves. Every one of us has places in our lives where we excel and other places where we are vulnerable. The apostle Paul said, "For through the grace given to me I say to everyone among you not to think more highly of himself than he ought to think; but to think so as to have sound judgment, as God has allotted to each a measure of faith" (Romans 12:3). Paul is not telling us that we should feel bad about ourselves; he is teaching us to understand the measure or *metron* of our faith. The Greek word *metron* means our place of influence or sphere of authority. We can always tell the size of our metron by the faith or confidence we have in our ability to complete a mission or accomplish a task. When we find ourselves feeling overwhelmed by circumstances or situations, it can be a sign that we have traveled outside our metron, exposing the low places of our walls.

I have watched many people try to take on someone else's metron, only to find themselves drowning in the storm-tossed seas of self-doubt and discouragement. But when we remain inside our own metron, we have faith for our calling that manifests as confidence in our God-given ability to fulfill our mission. Whether we are cleaning toilets or leading a country, we should never lose sight of the fact that whenever we are doing something for God, we are doing a *great* work that makes our life worth living. This sense of significance is a powerful weapon of warfare against the hordes of hell. Significance is an invisible force field that protects our confidence in God. It is a shield of faith for our souls. When we forget that what we are doing with our lives matters to God, we leave the gates of our hearts unguarded, accessible to enemy influence.

Remember Who You Are

Nehemiah was a master at discerning the enemy's plots and knowing how to defuse them. In the final round of Nehemiah's prize-winning fight with the devil, Nehemiah dodges the lying jabs of the enemy and lands the knockout punch when he reminds himself of who he is in the Lord:

When I entered the house of Shemaiah the son of Delaiah, son of Mehetabel, who was confined at home, he said, "Let us meet together in the house of God, within the temple, and let us close the doors of the temple, for they are coming to kill you, and they are coming to kill you at night." *But I said, "Should a man like me flee? And could one such as I go into the temple to save his life? I will not go in." Then I perceived that surely God had not sent him, but he uttered his prophecy against me because Tobiah and Sanballat had hired him.* He was hired for this reason, that I might become frightened and act accordingly and sin, so that they might have an evil report in order that they could reproach me. Remember, O my God, Tobiah and Sanballat according to these works of theirs, and also Noadiah the prophetess and the rest of the prophets who were trying to frighten me. So the wall was completed on the twenty-fifth of the month Elul, in fifty-two days. When all our enemies heard of it, and all the nations surrounding us saw it, they lost their confidence; for they recognized that this work had been accomplished with the help of our God.

Nehemiah 6:10–16, emphasis added

Self-importance will not withstand the enemy's assaults; in fact, pride comes before a fall. But true confidence in God's work in our lives shields us from the flaming arrows of fear, terror and torment. The goal of *all* enemy assaults is to scare us out of our divine destiny.

Many people "hide in the temple" by forming alliances with religious spirits, hoping they will protect them. Religious spirits inspire people to keep rules, formulas and laws to shield themselves from the onslaughts of demonic devices. But this is like asking the mafia to guard your business. Soon you will find yourself in an allegiance with the destroyer and will become his next victim. Of course, discipline is a good thing if it is inspired by the Holy Spirit and flows from intimacy with Him. But discipline inspired by religious spirits will lead you to put your trust in your own strength instead of His. Such disciplines are powerless against the enemy, for they are sponsored by evil spirits and will only lead to oppression in our lives.

It is important to note that it was only after Nehemiah reassured himself of his identity and refused to hide behind religious forms (the temple), that he had the discernment to recognize that God did not inspire the negative declarations made against him. Fear clouds our convictions and distorts our discernment. When we fill our minds with negative predictions or allow our thoughts to manipulate us into thinking about all the possible destructive outcomes of our mission, we invite fear to paralyze our progress. We also sin against God by not pressing forward to fulfill our call and accomplish our mission. But when we press past the intimidation of demonic spirits and commit even more resolutely to finishing our divine assignments, we torment the tormentors and they lose their confidence. Let's live to destroy the works of the devil and give him and his thugs a nervous breakdown.

In the next chapter, we will view warfare through the dark night of the soul and see if we can gain more insight into this powerful yet invisible realm.

4

The Wilderness

Moses sent Joshua, Caleb and ten others on a mission to spy out the Promised Land. They sighted giants in the midst of their God-given territory. Joshua and Caleb wanted to pick a fight with the giants and obtain their treasure, but the crowd preferred to reduce God's promise to the level of their fear.

The devil always stations giants right in the middle of our God-given purposes, and the Lord often endorses them. Remember Jesus' wilderness experience? It was the Holy Spirit who led Jesus into the wilderness to be tempted by the devil. It was God who was picking a fight with Satan. God lured the devil into a brawl by weakening the flesh of Christ with a forty-day fast. Then Jesus beat the devil at his own game. When you read the account in Matthew 3:16–4:11, you will notice that as soon as Jesus received God's divine endorsement in His identity and calling as the Son of God, He was led into the wilderness *by the Holy Spirit* to meet the devil in the mother of all battles. The Bible is pretty silent about the thirty years leading up to this confrontation—this appears to be the first major conflict Jesus encountered (unless you call His parents losing Him for three days stressful). But at His baptism, the preparation of those thirty years was complete, and the hour had come for Him to step into His assignment—to destroy the works of the devil and cast the "god of this world" off a stolen throne.

In the previous chapter, we saw the same pattern in Nehemiah's story. Before the report came from Jerusalem, his life was pretty simple. He lived in the king's palace and undoubtedly had all the perks that came with it. But that life was not where he would make his mark; it only prepared him by positioning him in the presence of the king. When the news of Jerusalem came, something woke up in Nehemiah. He realized that he was born to do more than hang out in the palace and sip suds with the king—he was called as the catalyst of a reformation that delivered his people from the clutches of an evil enemy and restored them to their former glory. But the first thing he encountered when he stepped into his destiny was an enemy attack over his identity. In the same way, Christ, after hearing His Father speak to Him from heaven about being His beloved Son, immediately encountered a demonic voice that questioned His identity as the Son of God. Hundreds of years separated Nehemiah and Jesus, but the demonic scheme remained the same.

I hope you are beginning to see a pattern here. The dogs of doom always lie waiting at the doors of our destiny. Between God's promises in our life and the palace of our divine purpose is always the process that molds us into the person we need to be to stay seated in the palace. Joseph Garlington said, "God closes one door and opens another, but it's hell in the hallway." It is in the "hallway" that we need to remember the words of the great apostle Paul, who was intimately acquainted with "hallway" experiences. He wrote, "Thanks be to God, who always leads us in triumph in Christ" (2 Corinthians 2:14). We often quote verses like this, but we forget that there is no victory without a battle, no testimony without a test and no miracle without an impossible circumstance. God leads us in triumph by leading us into battles, tests and impossibilities! It was the Holy Spirit who led Jesus into the wilderness, God who inspired Nehemiah to rebuild the walls, and it is Jesus who led you to read this book because you were born to change the world!

Of course, two agendas are always operating in any war. Often when we find ourselves in these epic battles in the wilderness, where our souls are being tested to their limits, we ask whether it was God or the devil who led us there. The answer is yes—God and the devil both have a plan for us in the "dark night of the soul," though they intend entirely different outcomes. The question is, with whose plan will we side? It is only after we have faced the devil alone in the wilderness, believed God and won our personal victory that the Lord can trust us with any kind of public promotion.

Temptation and Sin

A misunderstanding of the difference between temptation and sin has caused many people to believe they are losing their wilderness battles, when actually they are winning. The writer of Hebrews said that Christ was "tempted in all things as we are, yet without sin" (Hebrews 4:15). It is important for us to understand that temptation is not sin. For something to tempt us, we have to have a natural desire for it. For example, if I had not eaten all day and you left me alone in a room with a platter of sushi, it would not tempt me because I hate sushi. On the other hand, if I were hungry and you set a nice, hot, juicy lobster tail in front of me, I would be tempted! We cannot be tempted with something we have no desire for. That is why the devil tempted Jesus with "turn these stones into bread"—he knew Jesus had not eaten in forty days. It was the fact that Jesus was hungry that made the suggestion a temptation.

You are probably asking yourself, *When does a temptation become a sin?* Temptation becomes a sin when you agree with the suggestion instead of resisting it. If a beautiful, naked woman ran out in front of a crowd, every normal man in the mob would be tempted because God gave men a sex drive. But it is not until they choose to agree with the temptation that they have sinned. If one of the men in the crowd said to himself, *I really would like to have sex with that woman*, now he has crossed over the line of temptation and entered the world of sin. Even though at that point he has done nothing physically wrong, he has already sinned in his heart.

I recently had a conversation with a high-profile leader who told me that he sinned every day. I was stunned. When I asked what he meant by *sin*, he began to describe several different temptations that he faced from day to day.

"Do you agree with those temptations in your mind when they come up in your heart?" I questioned.

"No, of course I don't. I know better than that," was his answer.

"Then you haven't sinned, you've only been tempted. Temptation is not sin," I explained.

The leader was shocked by the true definition of sin. In that moment, that person was set free from a lifetime of guilt over feeling as though he had continually failed the Lord.

Strength in Weakness

It is important to point out here that the devil left Jesus alone until "an opportune time." Satan is an opportunist. He often strategically waits to attack until we are hungry, weak or tired. Although the devil is insane, he is not stupid. But the Holy Spirit is the most brilliant strategist. He knew that the easiest way to draw Satan into His trap was to weaken Jesus. The plan worked perfectly!

Christ's main strategy in the wilderness was to fast. It seems crazy to put yourself in a place of hunger, weakness and vulnerability before going up against an enemy—unless you understand that the goal of the wilderness is to uncover God's unfailing ability to deliver you. That is why Jesus fasted. He wanted to remove any temptation that He might have to try to defeat the devil in His own strength. All that was left after forty days was a choice—God's strength, or the devil's false offer of power. In His weakness, Jesus simply refused to listen to the devil and fully entrusted Himself to God. As Jude said, God "is able to keep you from stumbling, and to make you stand in the presence of His glory blameless with great joy" (Jude 24). It is our responsibility to trust God. It is His responsibility to deliver, protect and save us.

An old saying continually circulates throughout the Body of Christ: "Greater levels, greater devils." The adage basically means that every time God promotes someone, He exposes them to more demonic assaults. Entire Christian camps actually believe that sickness, relational conflict and troubles are a sign that you have been promoted. What these folks fail to realize is that when God promotes you, He protects you.

Just think about it: The most protected person in the United States is our president. He receives the protection at the same time he receives the promotion. Nobody in his right mind would take the office of the presidency without the protection the promotion deserves. How much better does God, who has legions of angels at His disposal, protect the people He promotes? Of course nobody, no matter their status in the Kingdom, is immune from the troubles of life or the weaknesses of their own personhood. That is why Paul wrote,

> He has said to me, "My grace is sufficient for you, for power is perfected in weakness." Most gladly, therefore, I will rather boast about my weaknesses, so that the power of Christ may dwell in me. Therefore I am well content with weaknesses, with insults, with distresses, with persecutions, with difficulties, for Christ's sake; for when I am weak, then I am strong.
>
> 2 Corinthians 12:9–10

God does not want our confidence to be in our own ability. Philippians 3:3 puts it this way: "For we are the true circumcision, who worship in the Spirit of God and glory in Christ Jesus and put no confidence in the flesh." It is vital that we put our confidence entirely in the work God has done in us. Self-righteousness or any assurances that are not rooted in Christ will only lead to temporary solutions that always backfire.

The clear purpose of wilderness battles is to test and establish our faith. The apostle James told us to rejoice in trials because of what they produce in us—the same maturity and perfection that Christ displayed in His complete dependence on God.

> Consider it all joy, my brethren, when you encounter various trials, knowing that the *testing of your faith* produces endurance. And let endurance have its perfect result, so that you may be perfect and complete, lacking in nothing.
>
> James 1:2–4, emphasis added

Did you notice that trials do not test our character, they test our faith? Faith is fundamentally a relational term—it is not first a matter of *what* you believe, but of *whom* you trust. The battle for our trust is as old as Adam and Eve. In the midst of battle, it can seem so complex, but when the dust settles and the smoke clears, the real war is always over the same question—*whom will we believe?* Whom will we listen to, God or the devil?

When Adam and Eve sinned in the Garden, they did not just disobey God . . . they obeyed Satan. Regarding the Tree of Knowledge of Good and Evil, the Lord had said, "You shall not eat from it or touch it, or you will die." But the devil had said, "You surely will not die!" (Genesis 3:3–4). They chose to obey the devil instead of God and eat from the wrong tree. When they made that choice, they changed masters. Trials are designed to help us determine who our master will be, whom we will trust, who our Lord will be and which kingdom we will put our faith in.

75

Do We Live in Fear or Peace?

Most of us would probably argue that we would never trust the devil. But it might not occur to us that putting our faith in anyone or anything besides God creates only symptomatic cures and is actually idolatry. An idol is anything you trust more than you trust God, or anything you have to check with before you say yes to God.

In my own life, I have struggled at times with the fear of death. If I have some negative physical symptom, I immediately go to the doctor to find out what is wrong and what can be done to help cure me. Let me clearly state that I am in no way opposed to seeing a doctor when you are sick. Jesus Himself said that those who are sick need a physician (see Matthew 9:12). But after all the tests are run and the results are in, we still have to decide if we will trust God or man.

It is so important that we do not confuse the facts with the truth. Physicians, for example, are trained to give us the facts. It is their job to diagnose our condition and identify the best treatment based on their training, experience and the available information. But the truth—what God says about a situation or condition—overrides the facts. A doctor should never have the final word, therefore, on our condition or treatment. We must always consult the Great Physician and be guided by His prognosis before we ever subject ourselves to the medical profession.

We often fear the worst when we visit the doctor or find ourselves in some other situation in which we feel powerless. The apostle John wrote, "There is no fear in love; but perfect love casts out fear, because fear involves punishment, and the one who fears is not perfected in love" (1 John 4:18). Think about it—if our Daddy is God and He made everything in the universe simply by speaking it into existence, and He happens to love us enough to send His Son to die for us, then it stands to reason that worry is completely irrational!

Is it not true that all anxiety, fear and torment in a Christian's life can be traced back to the fact that we have forgotten who we are and/or whose we are? This brings us back to what we learned from the life of Nehemiah and the temptation of Christ in the wilderness. In both cases, the enemy's devious strategy was to try to get them questioning who they were.

If you are dealing with anxiety, torment, fear, low self-esteem, depression or any other negative emotion, it is very likely that you have forgotten that the Creator of the universe loves you. Do not entertain the enemy's questions about how valuable you are. As Pastor Bill Johnson says, "Any thought that does not inspire hope is rooted in a lie." Let's stop believing lies! Let's embrace the truth and live in peace.

5

The Flesh Is Weak

We humans are complex creatures. The triune nature of our being creates a beautiful, intricate ecosystem of spirit, soul and body. When that ecosystem functions according to God's design, it is like poetry in motion. In fact, Paul said, "We are His workmanship, created in Christ Jesus for good works" (Ephesians 2:10). The Greek word for "workmanship" is *poiema*, from which we derive our English word *poem*. In other words, we humans are God's poem. God spoke, and we became His living message to a desperate and dying world. Paul also wrote,

> You are our letter, written in our hearts, known and read by all men; being manifested that you are a letter of Christ, cared for by us, written not with ink but with the Spirit of the living God, not on tablets of stone but on tablets of human hearts.
>
> 2 Corinthians 3:2–3

What an awesome picture of the eternal love of our Creator.

Sometimes, however, our complex triune ecosystem malfunctions, and God's poem no longer rhymes. His song begins to be sung off-key in us, so to speak. In the previous chapters, we explored the spiritual dimension of our triune being and the effect that the demonic realm can have on our personhood. In this chapter, I want to share something I learned the hard way a few years ago about the physical side of our triune being.

The Dark Night of the Flesh

A terrible experience I went through reinforced the fact that even as Christians, our physical dimension—our flesh—is still weak. It is no longer evil, but it is weak. As Jesus said to His disciples who kept falling asleep when He had asked them to watch and pray, "The spirit is willing, but the flesh is weak" (Matthew 26:41). This was revealed to me in a new way, beginning with a conversation I had with Bill Johnson's secretary, Judy. She called to tell me Bill was very sick, and the doctors ordered him to cancel all his travel so that he could rest for a couple of months.

"Bill asked that you take as many of his conferences as you can while he is ill," Judy requested.

I already had a full travel schedule of my own, but Judy and I sat down together and figured out a way that I could fly from conference to conference to cover most of Bill's speaking engagements without missing any of mine. For nearly two months, I was flying all over the place; from state to state . . . country to country . . . time zone to time zone. My body's internal clock got so messed up that I could not sleep much no matter where I was.

One day in the midst of this whirlwind of activity, somewhere in Australia, I was preparing to take the pulpit to speak when my cell phone rang. My caller ID identified the caller as a very close family member. I asked my host to postpone my introduction, and I stepped out into the lobby to answer the call.

"Are you all right?" I questioned.

"No! I'm having panic attacks and I'm totally freaked out!" the family member told me.

I tried to comfort her, but there was no time to really get to the root of her fear right then. When I finished preaching, I called again and we talked deep into the night. I tried to help the person work through her irrational fears. That first phone call turned into several conversations per day as I crisscrossed the world doing conferences. I was completely physically and emotionally exhausted, and I was so tired that my imagination started to go wild with what-if thoughts. I would lie awake at night envisioning my loved one committing suicide or being put in a mental hospital. How could this be happening? Had I failed her in some way?

My head was spinning. I was frazzled, but it is very hard not to answer the phone when your family needs help. I had to both maintain my heavy schedule and take time to walk through this with the person. Bill was still recovering, and I felt as though the weight of the world was on my shoulders.

About three months into this nightmare, my son, who is a pastor on our staff, came into my office. He looked panicked.

"What's wrong?" I questioned.

"Dad, I think my marriage is over!" he said, covering his face with his hands.

"No, son!" I protested. "God can work this out."

But it was not to be . . . after ten years and three children, his marriage was over. Jason was a mess after that. It took almost two years for him to recover. Although he went through a divorce, he and the kids are doing great now. (You can read our co-authored book *The Supernatural Power of Forgiveness*[1] for the continuation of his story.) Jason's situation, however, came alongside everything else I was already dealing with at the time. Although I was completely exhausted by then, I could not sleep. I would lay awake all night imagining worst-case scenarios. How would the kids survive this divorce? What if my son had a nervous breakdown? How were we going to tell our church that Jason, one of the senior leaders of our ministry school, was going through a divorce? Speculations plagued my mind.

As days turned into weeks, my anxiety grew. Soon the anxiety was compounded by panic attacks that occurred several times a day. I was almost completely incapacitated. The war going on in my soul preoccupied my mind to the point that I could hardly think of anything else. Every little thing bothered me. Anxiety so gripped my soul that I began to fear leaving the house.

But the worst was yet to come. One day I woke up to the feeling that someone had dropped me into a deep black hole. I began to despair of life itself, and I lost the will to live. I lost my appetite for food, sex or anything that I usually love to do. In the three months that followed, I lost 35 pounds. I was so depressed that I could hardly get off the couch. I saw several counselors, including a couple of professionals, but nothing made much difference.

I was so desperate that I was willing to do anything to make the depression lift. I finally agreed to take my doctor's advice to try antidepressant medication (I call her my doctor, but she is actually a nurse practitioner). I was allergic to the first four drugs she prescribed, so it took a couple of months before I began to improve at all. The doctor also prescribed medication to help me sleep.

It took me months to agree to take anything to relieve my symptoms. I was so afraid of what people would think of me if they knew I was on mind-meds. I was also very confused about why God did not deliver me. Was this a demon of depression? Was I in some sort of secret sin? Was I mentally ill? Would this ever end? Was I going to have to take medication for the rest of my life? My mind kept spinning.

The medicine caused some uncomfortable side effects like hot flashes and cold sweats. It also made me feel emotionally numb. But the deep depression and anxiety lifted considerably, and I was able to function fairly normally. About four months into taking the antidepressant, I talked with a friend about my symptoms and condition. He told me that many years earlier he had suffered the same symptoms, and after several tests, the doctor finally discovered that he had a hormone imbalance. I went back to my doctor and asked her to run a test on my testosterone levels. She did not really think that was my problem, but she agreed to do another blood test. A couple days later, we got the results back. I had almost no testosterone in my system whatsoever. She immediately prescribed testosterone. Within sixty days, I was able to stop taking the antidepressants and the sleeping pills. After a ten-month journey through hell, I finally felt completely normal again.

What I Learned in Hell

During my ten-month journey through hell, I read every book on anxiety and depression that I could get my hands on. I discovered that while there are many differing opinions on the subject of mental health, most scientists agree on a few common themes. I learned that literally hundreds of chemical reactions go on in our brains at any given time. These chemical interactions play a major role in the way we feel, think and behave. Most scientists agree that the chemical compound called serotonin acts as a neurotransmitter and is the principal catalyst for mental and emotional health. Antidepressants like Prozac artificially stimulate serotonin production in our bodies and help balance the brain's chemistry when there is a deficiency. (I should note here that other important neurotransmitters like dopamine and norepinephrine can affect mood as well. Medications are also available to help people who suffer from an imbalance in these neurotransmitter systems.)

Most scientists believe that four primary factors affect the *natural* stimulation of serotonin production in our bodies. These factors are sleep, sunlight, stress and exercise. It is interesting to note how negatively these factors have been affected in the last century. For example, a recent study revealed that since the invention of the lightbulb, the average person sleeps an hour less a night. I would add that television, the Internet and entertainment in general are also incentives that generate excitement and cause us to stay up much later and sleep less.

The second factor that plays a major role is the amount of time we spend in the sun—or do not spend in it. Since we transitioned from the agricultural age to the information age, many more people live and work indoors. Simply stated, people in developed countries just do not spend as much time outside as their ancestors did.

Stress is the third factor in serotonin production. The average person today is exposed to more bad news in one week than someone just fifty years ago heard in a year. Add to this that it is almost impossible to rest in our culture. There are so many ways to get in touch with people—cell phones, voice mail, email, text messaging, pagers, Skype, iChat, social networking . . . the list is nearly endless. The information age makes it nearly impossible to take a break from people. Then there is the time clock. Our daily schedules are planned around minutes. There are 1440 minutes in a day, and for most of us, every one them is spoken for months in advance. To make matters worse, while we are in any given meeting, we are usually being texted, called or paged, making it impossible to fully concentrate on the task at hand. Add to this that most of us have jobs that do not require much brawn, but that tax our brains to the max all day long. No wonder we are wound up so tight all the time.

Probably the factor having the greatest negative effect on our mental state, though, is the cultural shift in the transportation industry. With the invention of cars, planes and trains, people walk much less. We get only a fraction of the exercise people got just a hundred years ago. Think about it. How many people do you think worked out at a gym in the agricultural age? There was no need for that given the physical challenges of their daily lives!

If it is true that these four factors—sleep, sunlight, stress and exercise—are the primary catalysts for serotonin production in our brains, then it does not take a genius to figure out why so many people are taking antidepressants to feel normal in this generation.

What makes hormone imbalances even more complex is that serotonin cannot be measured. There is no blood test, or any other test for that matter, that you can take to determine the level of serotonin in your brain. Serotonin reproduction remains somewhat of a mystery, and the science of it remains subjective. For example, there is some debate over serotonin and sleep interaction. Does a person's lack of sleep result in reduced serotonin levels? Or does serotonin somehow become low in a person's body first, which then causes the person to lose sleep?

Professionals hold various opinions concerning the catalytic nature of brain chemistry. Add to this that scientific breakthroughs are happening nearly every day in this field, and some of them will probably supersede the data in this chapter before this book hits the market. But suffice to say that body chemistry is a vitally important factor in the well-being of our spirit, soul and body.

Tri-Polar Thinking

In my season from hell I learned that our spirit, soul and body are so intricately intertwined that it is impossible to affect one part without directly or indirectly influencing the other two parts. Take, for example, the color purple. We all know that purple is not a primary color; it is the result of mixing blue and red together. But once red and blue are blended, I defy you ever to separate them again. Our triune being is similar. We often talk about the spirit, soul and body as if they live in separate boxes, but the reality is that life does not really happen that way for any of us. Our triune ecosystem flows together in a complex series of interactions. Problems can originate or be rooted in one dimension of our being, but before long, we experience resulting symptoms in all three realms of our personhood.

In my book *Developing a Supernatural Lifestyle*,[2] I shared that God showed me it was His desire to heal the whole person. Consider the case study of the lame man at the gate Beautiful in the book of Acts:

> But Peter said, "I do not possess silver and gold, but what I do have I give to you: In the name of Jesus Christ the Nazarene—walk!" And seizing him by the right hand, he raised him up; and immediately his feet and his ankles were strengthened. With a leap he stood upright and began to walk; and he entered the temple with them, *walking and leaping and praising God*.
>
> Acts 3:6–8, emphasis added

The man walked because he got physically healed. He leaped because he got emotionally healed. And he praised God because he got spiritually restored! When one dimension of our triune being is sick, it affects our entire being. When we understand this, it makes sense that the Lord works to restore the whole person. Merely healing our bodies would be only a temporary, partial solution.

If we and those we minister to are going to come into true wholeness, it is essential that we understand how these triune systems interact with each other and how this affects our lives and the health of our whole being. When I crashed, I could not figure out what was wrong with me because my symptoms were multidimensional. My soul was in deep grief, my body was exhausted and my spirit was under constant assault. The turmoil over *where* my problem originated was so confusing that it literally accounted for half my stress.

Thinking from the Spirit

Over time, I came to realize that our brains receive information from three sources. The first source of influence on our thinking is our spirit. Paul said, "Be renewed in the spirit of your mind" (Ephesians 4:23). In other words, we have the ability to think from the spirit of our mind. We know that if someone has an evil spirit, it affects the way they think. Whether they are demonized or just under spiritual attack, enemy combatants are influencing their thoughts. (We spoke of this in previous chapters.)

Our spirit deals with the dark world all the time because Jesus said the accuser of the brethren is hammering away at our spirit day and night (see Revelation 12:10). Because God designed us to be spiritually resilient, most of the time we are unaware that this level of negativity is happening around us until our spirit needs to get our attention so that we can proactively resist these forces.

When it needs reinforcements, one of the main ways our spirit communicates with our conscious mind is through dreams. A dream that we are being chased but can only run in slow motion is often our spirit's way of telling us it needs our help to prevail against enemy agents. We may need to fast, pray more or focus on some aspect of spiritual warfare that aids our spirit in warding off a demonic attack.

Thinking from the Body

We are all aware that certain chemicals, foods and sleep habits affect our physical or natural mind. If we do not get enough sleep or if we take certain drugs, it affects the way we think. Our natural mind is also quite busy orchestrating an entire ecosystem that is literally keeping us alive. It is accomplishing all of this below the conscious level.

It is amazing that our natural mind runs our entire body while we rarely even think about it. Our natural mind has an army at its disposal so that anytime any kind of biological warfare comes against our physical being, it deploys millions of soldiers called antibodies into combat for us. Our natural mind knows things that it does not make us conscious of unless it needs our input. But if our body encounters a battle that requires our attention, it sends us a signal in the form of pain so that we can participate in dealing with the illness. If we break a leg, our natural mind knows that it cannot heal the break without making us aware that we need to stop walking on the leg long enough for our body to repair it from the inside out. Our natural mind therefore sends us a message in the form of pain that says, "Hey, buddy, get off of that leg while we are working on it!"

Thinking from the Soul

Our soul is the third member of our triune being. We often call this dimension of thinking "processing from the heart." I am fully convinced that our heart (soul) knows things that the other two elements are completely unaware of. The heart feels its way through life and is sensitive to emotions.

From the soul comes the intangible, illogical, but often most important essentials of our being. The soul is the home where things like love, passion and mercy live. If, for example, someone hurts your feelings or a person close to you dies, it affects the way you think. Your soul deals with hurts and disappointments all the time. But when it gets overwhelmed and needs your help to heal, it often sends signals in the form of emotional pain such as depression, anger or grief. David said of the Lord, "He restores my soul" (Psalm 23:3).

The Triune Interaction

Our body, soul and spirit work interdependently, for they do not merely inhabit, but they cohabit our being. In 1 Samuel, Hannah was terribly troubled because she was unable to bear children. So she went to the temple to pray, and she caused so much drama while praying one day that Eli the priest thought she was drunk. But Hannah replied, "No, my lord, I am a woman oppressed in *spirit*; I have drunk neither wine nor strong drink, but I have poured out my *soul* before the LORD" (1 Samuel 1:15, emphasis added). Note that she was grieved in her spirit, but she poured out her soul. This is a beautiful example of the interdependent relationship between the soul and the spirit. Her root issue was she was oppressed in her spirit, but it was also affecting her soul.

I can look back on my crash now and understand that although my depression affected me emotionally and spiritually, it actually was rooted in the physical dimension of my mind and body. I ignored several warning signs my mind was sending me months before I completely crashed and burned. I was exhausted, but I kept pushing myself, rationalizing that I had no choice. Many days, I would lie on the floor during worship, right before I was to speak, and fall asleep. I got so tired of ministering to people that I resented them. I was continually overwhelmed with the thought that I had nothing more to give. Making any decision during that time created anxiety in me. Yet I ignored all the warning signs, and soon I was physically, emotionally and spiritually a basket case.

I had known stress, anxiety and warfare before, but this was so intense that I could not will myself off the couch no matter how hard I tried. Unlike the demonic attack that I experienced years earlier, this crash was rooted in my body. I lay there completely incapacitated for nearly three months. People from all over the world prayed for me and encouraged me. But until my body chemistry stabilized, I could not function.

I have to confess that I have *never* believed in taking antidepressants. When I preached, I had actually made light of people who used them. I still do not think they are the long-term cure for many people. I think that they can often mask deeper issues in our lives. Antidepressant medications, however, can have a role in helping people function. Some people who suffer from chronic neurotransmitter deficiencies are helped tremendously by such medications. Many healthcare professionals believe that either due to brain injury or genetic predisposition, some people do not have the physical ability to regulate brain chemistry levels normally.

If you think about it, we would never tell people in the church who have diabetes that if they would just spend more time with God or pray more, they could stop taking their insulin (unless, of course, God heals them). Yet that is what we suggest to people whose chemical imbalances have a physical cause. Even though our brain is an organ just like our pancreas, we view mood disorders that are rooted in our physical being in a much less accepting manner.

I think we need to extend more grace to people in this area. You cannot understand how intense depression and anxiety can be unless you have been there, and not every chemical imbalance signifies a demon. Sometimes we need to give people permission to take medication if they need it—which, by the way, is a *huge* no-no in many Christian circles. Often these people are made to feel ashamed for taking such medication. As a result, they wait far longer than they should to get a doctor's help, and they delay their healing. I know because I am one of them. I was encouraged by caring, well-meaning people *not* to take medication, but after months of hell and hundreds of hours of research, I decided I needed more medical attention. My goal in this chapter is to help you better understand our triune being and how each of our three parts affects the others, so that if you find yourself in a place like the one I was in, you can seek out the kind of help you need and be made whole.

Take Action!

My advice to anyone who has been dealing with high levels of depression, anxiety and exhaustion for long periods of time is to take action! I know that can seem impossible—it did to me. As I said, I did not move off the couch for three months. But you can do some things that will help you through.

First, visit a respected health care professional and have a complete physical, including blood work that incorporates hormone tests. If the physical part of your mind that regulates brain chemistry is malfunctioning, medical intervention is a necessity.

I also recommend that you read two other books. The first is *From Panic to Power* by Lucinda Bassett.[3] The second is *Who Switched Off My Brain? Controlling Toxic Thoughts and Emotions* by Dr. Caroline Leaf.[4] I have given away at least fifty of these books. They really helped me in my darkest hour. Both books contain a wealth of information about brain chemistry and how to detox your thought life.

Another important thing is to take care of your body now more than ever. Do what you have to do to sleep. Force yourself to exercise even when you do not feel like it. Eat healthy food even when you are not hungry. Stay completely away from sugar and caffeine. Get as much sunlight as possible, and try to stay busy.

Work hard at cultivating upbeat moments, too. Watch movies and do things that make you laugh a lot. Laughter is a natural medicine. Surround yourself with good friends who will support you in these troubled times. Believe the positive things they say about you, even if their words do not seem real to you.

Most importantly, pray for God to heal and restore you. Remember who you are and whose you are!

Lastly, I want to encourage you by letting you know that *this will pass.* In the last few years, I have met hundreds of people from all walks of life—including several world-famous people—who have passed through this kind of thing at some point in their lives. I know that when you are in the middle of it, your worst fear is, *Am I going to live like this my entire life?* The answer is no! This always passes. You *will* be fine!

6

Treating Yourself Kindly

One of the schemes evil spirits employ is to deceive people into believing that mistreating themselves is somehow spiritual. Many of these baffled believers are convinced that they please God when they think of themselves as losers, lowlifes or sinners. These believers have lost sight of Paul's words in Ephesians 5:29: "No one ever hated his own flesh, but nourishes and cherishes it, just as Christ also does the church." So it is about time we learn how to tenderly care for ourselves, because Jesus wants us to have a great life—spirit, soul and body.

When we live in anything less than righteousness, peace and joy, we are not experiencing everything that our Lord paid for. Jesus put it this way: "The thief comes only to steal and kill and destroy; I came that they may have life, and have it abundantly" (John 10:10). It is so important that we do not get the thief and the Lord mixed up! We have an enemy who is trying to deprive us of the benefits of the Kingdom. I talk more about this in my first book, *The Supernatural Ways of Royalty* (co-authored with Bill Johnson).[1]

The devil often finds an open door to condemn us when we do something wrong. The Lord convicts us when we sin. The difference between condemnation and conviction may seem subtle, but it can be deadly. Condemnation says, "You lied, therefore you are a liar. You got drunk, therefore you must be an alcoholic." Condemnation tries to convince us that our bad action is the fruit of being a bad person.

On the other hand, conviction says, "You are way too awesome to act like that." Conviction reminds us of our God-given identity and calls us to act like a son or daughter of God, not a sinner.

If we listen to the devil, he will convince us that we are bad people who deserve punishment. It is impossible to experience real joy while believing we are evil. Remember, when Jesus died on the cross for us, He changed our nature and we became part of the Royal Family. And as I said in chapter 3, Jesus became our advocate or lawyer, and it is important that we never talk to the devil without our attorney present. We also should not do for the devil what he cannot do for himself. He cannot touch us; he can only talk to us. So when we self-destruct, we are doing for the devil what he cannot do for himself.

Talking to Yourself

We are not sinners, but saints, and we must remind ourselves of our family status. One of the ways we nourish our new nature is to talk to ourselves regarding what God thinks about us. Whether we are young or old, male or female, introverted or extroverted, we have more conversations with ourselves than we have with anyone else in the world. I once heard Dr. Lance Wallnau, a recognized Christian leader in the field of personal and organizational transformation, cite a large university study revealing that the average person hears twelve hundred words a minute of self-talk. The study found that eleven hundred of these words are negative in most people! If you add to that the fact that we tend to trust ourselves more than anyone else, what do you think happens when we speak negatively, punish or talk down to ourselves? What happens is that we destroy our own confidence, kill our self-esteem and ultimately end up in the boneyard of depression, hopelessness and fear.

On the other hand, when we take the Word and the thoughts of God and begin to speak them into our new man, we start to experience the fruit of the Spirit in the depths of our very beings. Peace starts saturating our minds, joy infiltrates our souls and the life of God is released into our mortal bodies.

One of the greatest examples of this principle is hidden in the life of the Old Testament character Joshua. In the most challenging season of his life, he learned one of the most important lessons of his life. As I describe the circumstances, see if you can relate to his situation.

God had just told Joshua that Moses, his leader and personal hero, was dead. To make matters even more challenging, the Lord also informed him that the divine mission Moses failed to fulfill was now being assigned to him! Joshua must have felt alone, scared, discouraged and overwhelmed. In the face of all that, God gave him these instructions:

> Be strong and courageous, for you shall give this people possession of the land which I swore to their fathers to give them. Only be strong and very courageous; be careful to

do according to all the law which Moses My servant commanded you; do not turn from it to the right or to the left, so that you may have success wherever you go. This book of the law shall not depart from your mouth, but you shall meditate on it day and night, so that you may be careful to do according to all that is written in it; for then you will make your way prosperous, and then you will have success. Have I not commanded you? Be strong and courageous! Do not tremble or be dismayed, for the LORD your God is with you wherever you go.

Joshua 1:6–9

Notice how God gave Joshua the secret of controlling his emotions and guaranteeing his victory. There are three keys here that God said would determine his success. First, the Law of God was to be in his mouth. Next, he was to meditate on it day and night. And finally, he was to do all that he was talking about and meditating on. It is interesting that the word *meditate* in this passage actually means to utter, muse, ponder, declare and even sing over yourself! In other words, God instructed Joshua to do more than just think about His Law; He actually commanded Joshua to talk, declare, muse and sing to himself about God's Word.

Like Joshua, when we come into an intense and challenging season in our lives, it often takes more than the simple memorizing of Scripture to keep us out of discouragement, depression, panic and fear. Something powerful happens when we verbalize what God thinks and says about us. Even the world has discovered this secret. If you read most self-help books, often you will find a chapter on speaking kindly to yourself. Psychologists call this principle positive self-talk. They realize that to verbalize affirming and encouraging words over ourselves helps build confidence and self-esteem. But how much more powerful this principle is when instead of just declaring good stuff to ourselves, we repeat what God is saying about us!

Prophecy—God's Secret Weapon

Timothy was an amazing giant in the faith. He was Paul's right-hand man and the leader of the church at Ephesus, which might have been the greatest church in the entire New Testament. But Timothy struggled with fear. Before sending him to Corinth, Paul had to write ahead and ask them to not do anything that would scare Timothy. Look at Paul's exhortation to the Corinthians: "Now if Timothy comes, see that he is with you without cause to be afraid, for he is doing the Lord's work, as I also am" (1 Corinthians 16:10).

It is hard to imagine an apostle having to write ahead of someone as famous as Timothy to keep the people from stressing him out, but that is what happened. Paul then wrote a personal letter to Timothy to remind him of his awesome heritage in the faith and to teach him that the fear he was dealing with was an evil spirit, not just a human emotion:

> I call to remembrance the genuine faith that is in you, which dwelt first in your grandmother Lois and your mother Eunice, and I am persuaded is in you also. Therefore I remind you to stir up the gift of God, which is in you through the laying on of my hands. For God has not given us a spirit of fear, but of power and of love and of a sound mind.
>
> 2 Timothy 1:5–7, NKJV

Paul also instructed him, "No longer drink water exclusively, but use a little wine for the sake of your stomach and your frequent ailments" (1 Timothy 5:23). This is only a guess, but it probably makes sense that Timothy's stomach problems were directly related to his struggles with stress. Wine was most likely prescribed to calm him down a little.

It comforts me that Timothy struggled with fear, yet that did not disqualify him from his great call. For some reason, in seasons of intense conflict we often feel as if we are the only ones who have ever gone through such a thing before. We can feel alone, abandoned and isolated. But the truth is that "no temptation has overtaken you but such as is common to man" (1 Corinthians 10:13). There is nothing we can experience that others have not gone through already. There is no depth of fear, no intensity of panic, no dark hole of depression and no hold of discouragement that millions of others have not also experienced. We are not alone!

Prophecy is one of God's most destructive weapons against the lies of the enemy that isolate us and separate us from the Body. Prophecy is foretelling and forthtelling our future. Foretelling is history revealed before it happens, but forthtelling causes the future. Look at Paul's most powerful exhortation to Timothy: "This charge I commit to you, son Timothy, *according to the prophecies previously made concerning you, that by them you may wage the good warfare*, having faith and a good conscience" (1 Timothy 1:18–19, NKJV, emphasis added).

Foretelling Prophecy

We can wage war with prophetic declarations. I learned about the power of foretelling prophecy at the end of my nervous breakdown, which I described in the opening chapter of this book. Some brothers persuaded me to attend a men's retreat in the mountains, and a prophet named Dick Joyce was speaking. In the middle of his message, he stopped and looked out over the congregation as if he was trying to find someone. Suddenly, he pointed right at me and asked me to come forward. Seventy men watched as I timidly made my way to the front of the room. I was terrified, thinking he was going to reveal my horrible thoughts to the entire crowd. But instead, he began to prophesy to me about my future. He said, *"The Lord has called you to be a pillar in the house of God. You shall be a teacher and a pastor to His people. You will travel the world strengthening and encouraging the Body of Christ. You shall be a patriarch and your wife shall be a matriarch to the Church."*

The foretelling prophetic word went on and on about my high call, my great destiny and my incredible courage. I transcribed that prophetic word and carried it in my pocket for years. Anytime I began to feel anxious, afraid or discouraged, I would read that prophetic word over myself out loud. That word became my favorite weapon of warfare against the onslaughts of the enemy. Like Timothy, I was both called to greatness and plagued by fear. I came to realize that fear was an evil spirit assigned to keep me from completing my God-given assignment. Meditating on the prophetic words spoken over our lives reminds us of God's desire for our future and His *ability* to fulfill our destiny.

Forthtelling Prophecy

Forthtelling prophecy does not just predict the future, it *causes* the future. The book of Ezekiel gives us a great example of this forthtelling principle. The prophet Ezekiel is taken to an ancient battlefield where the entire valley is covered with the dry bones of soldiers who died in battle. Then the Lord commands the prophet to prophesy life to the dry bones. As Ezekiel speaks life to the bones, a mighty army suddenly rises out of the dusty boneyard (see Ezekiel 37:1–10).

This forthtelling prophetic dimension actually calls things that are not as though they are. In the same way that God spoke the worlds into existence, these prophetic words become new worlds of His divine invention.

Prophecy is like a nuclear weapon in the hands of a believer. It is important that we embrace the kind of prophetic culture that calls out our destiny and reminds us of God's work in our lives. If we despise, reject or do not believe in prophecy, we play into the enemy's hands by laying down a vitally important weapon of our warfare.

Speaking Death

Ezekiel spoke to a boneyard, and a mighty army emerged. But Solomon said life and *death* are in the power of the tongue (see Proverbs 18:21). It is also possible, therefore, to take a mighty army and reduce it to a pile of bones through an untamed tongue! Look at the warning James gave us about shooting off our big mouths:

> Look at the ships also, though they are so great and are driven by strong winds, are still directed by a very small rudder wherever the inclination of the pilot desires. So also the tongue is a small part of the body, and yet it boasts of great things. See how great a forest is set aflame by such a small fire!
>
> James 3:4–5

Our tongue is like the rudder of a ship. It can steer us into a safe harbor until the winds of adversity pass us by. But instead of navigating our ship into a suitable refuge in the storms of life, we often tend to let go of the wheel. This allows the waves of circumstance to drive the rudder instead of our stances, virtues and values.

It is tough enough to be in such an intense battle that you cannot see the forest for the trees. But it is stupid to set the forest on fire with our tongues. One of the worst things we can do when we are battling the enemy's onslaughts and our mind is under siege is to speak. I do not mean we should avoid asking for help or grow silent in some corner; I am talking about verbalizing the demonic thoughts, speculations or lofty things being propagated against us. Articulating these poisonous arrows only helps assimilate them into our hearts and live them out in our souls.

Sometimes it is necessary in a counseling situation to share with a wise person what is going on in our minds so we can get to the root cause of our conflict. But otherwise, walking around repeating what is being spoken against us in the unseen realm only helps reinforce these lies in our own hearts. Politicians and marketing gurus understand the "principle of repetition" very well. This principle says, "People tend to believe what they hear repeated, whether it is true or not." Think about that—it is possible to talk yourself to *death*!

Planting Orchards

One day in my freshman year of high school, we had a substitute teacher in history class. Instead of teaching history, this substitute decided to read the palms of all the students in the room. I was young and did not understand the significance of what was released through divining, so I stood in line to get my palm read with the rest of my fellow students. When it was my turn, the teacher looked at my palm, sighed deeply and refused to read it.

I left the class distraught. My head was spinning. All I could do was think, *Why wouldn't she read my palm?* At the end of the day, I went back and begged her to read my palm. She reluctantly grabbed my hand and began to tell me what she saw.

"Your lifeline ends early. That means you will die very young," she said in a timid voice.

My face turned pale and my body shook uncontrollably as my thoughts swirled around in my head. I hurried out of her class and ran most of the way home. Her words haunted me for years. I gestated her destructive seeds, and they finally germinated when I crashed the year after I was married, as I described earlier. Bad words are like eating fruit from a poison tree. The deadly fruit of destructive words encompasses us every day. It is up to us not to consume and assimilate these words by allowing them to take root in our minds and hearts. Paul put it this way:

> Finally, brethren, whatever is true, whatever is honorable, whatever is right, whatever is pure, whatever is lovely, whatever is of good repute, if there is any excellence and if anything worthy of praise, dwell on these things. The things you have learned and received and heard and seen in me, practice these things, and the God of peace will be with you.
>
> Philippians 4:8–9

Bill Johnson says, "We can't afford to have a thought in our mind that isn't in His!" We must set up guards at the entrance of our hearts and minds to protect the Kingdom of God within ourselves. Meditating on negative words is like opening up our heart gate and allowing enemy armies to invade the peaceful palace of our souls. Our eyes and ears are two of the main gateways to our souls. It is vital that we steward what we hear and see so that seeds of deception do not get planted in the soil of our souls.

Testimonies Open Our Eyes

On the other hand, testimonies of God's supernatural acts are like planting God's seeds in our hearts. (I guess you could say God's deeds are heart seeds.) In Bill Johnson's bestselling book *Strengthen Yourself in the Lord: How to Release the Hidden Power of God in Your Life*,[2] Bill reminds us how testimonies become highways to our divine calling. In fact, the book of Revelation says, "The testimony of Jesus is the spirit of prophecy" (Revelation 19:10).

In other words, what God did for someone else, He will do for you. When we forget the works of God, we lose sight of His supernatural ability to rescue us from any situation no matter how desperate the circumstances. The sons of Ephraim are a great example of what happens when you spend all your energy preparing for battle in the visible realm, but ignore the unseen dimension of the spirit.

> The sons of Ephraim were archers equipped with bows, yet they turned back in the day of battle. They did not keep the covenant of God and refused to walk in His law; *they forgot His deeds and His miracles that He had shown them.*
>
> Psalm 78:9–11, emphasis added

These famous warriors forgot the miracles that God had accomplished in their lives and retreated in battle.

At Bethel Church, we work hard to not forget God's work in the life of our church body. A full-time staff member oversees a whole team of people who keep track of the miracles that take place through the ministry of our congregation. It is our desire to steward testimonies the way that some people steward property or finances. We proactively recount the works God has done so that we can remind ourselves of the miracles He is about to do. Moses instructed us to keep the commandments *and* the testimonies (see Deuteronomy 6:17).

Testimonies not only remind us of the miracles of God, they are meant to open our eyes to another realm of Kingdom provision. This principle was brought to light so clearly when the disciples forgot to bring bread on a boat trip (see Matthew 16:5–12). Jesus said to them, "Watch out and beware of the leaven of the Pharisees and Sadducees" (verse 6). The disciples were convinced that He was scolding them for being irresponsible with their provision. Jesus reminded them that He fed five thousand people with five loaves and four thousand people with seven loaves, and both times several baskets of bread were left over. Therefore, He said, "How is it that you do not understand that I did not speak to you concerning bread? But beware of the leaven of the Pharisees and Sadducees" (verse 11).

In other words, when they witnessed the miracle of Jesus multiplying the loaves (He multiplied fish also, but they were only arguing about bread), it was supposed to unveil another dimension of provision for them so that they never had to worry about being short of bread again. The testimony of the supernatural provision was to give them faith to see God in a new way. Yet they forgot the miracle of multiplication, which ultimately opened a door for worry, fear and anxiety to take root in their lives.

At Bethel Church, we begin every meeting with testimonies of God's miraculous intervention that we have witnessed in our circumstances. This creates an atmosphere of expectation that the challenges we face every day will be met with God's ability, not ours. We often spend up to an hour sharing testimonies at our monthly board meeting, where finances are the most common subject. You can feel the burden lift and faith rise in your heart as different leaders share their stories. When we finally "get down to business," we approach Bethel's practical problems with God's supernatural solutions in mind.

Like the sons of Ephraim, we should enter spiritual battles fully equipped with weapons of warfare. But we must not forget God's past victories in our lives, or we will lose heart and retreat in the heat of the battle. For years I have kept a journal to help me remember past victories. I am not very disciplined about writing in it every day, but in tough seasons I always record my struggles. In hard times, I go back and read the notes I made about my past fears and God's deliverances in my life. Lamentations 3:21 says, "This I recall to my mind, therefore I have hope." Recalling the work the Lord has done in our past really helps bring peace to us in our present stormy seasons.

Prepare Your Mind for Action

Sometimes through his plots and schemes, the enemy can create circumstances that promote storms in our lives. It is important that we prepare our minds for action so we do not get caught off guard and fall for his evil devices (see 1 Peter 1:13). I experienced this firsthand in 2004 when I had a serious colon problem. After more than a year of bleeding quite severely, I decided to see a doctor. I hate going to physicians because I have an irrational fear that they will find something terminally wrong with me. But I finally mustered up the courage to make an appointment.

For what seemed like an eternity, I sat in a cold, sterile examination room at the doctor's office by myself. As I waited impatiently, horrible images flooded my mind. I saw myself lying on an operating table with doctors surrounding me. They were all shaking their heads in distress. When the doctor finally arrived, I wanted to run out of the room. Instead, I shared my symptoms with him, playing them down so as not to alarm him. After an invasive examination (I will spare you the details), he concluded that I should see a specialist for a colonoscopy.

"A specialist!" I protested. "Can't you just give me a shot or a pill . . . or something?"

"No!" the doctor snapped back. "This could be minor, or it could be something serious!"

He tried to explain the test to me, but I was drunk with fear by then. I left his office with my head spinning. Of course, the specialist could not see me for two weeks! The next day I left to do a conference in Los Angeles. The host pastors picked Kathy and me up at the airport and took us out to lunch before the first meeting. We sat at the table in a nice restaurant and made small talk. I also sat fighting off panic as visions of my graveside funeral pressed into my mind. The waiter came over to take our drink order. He looked as troubled as I felt, so I decided to console him.

"How are you doing?" I asked.

"Not good," he responded without hesitation.

"What's bothering you?" I persisted.

"My brother died of colon cancer last week. I just returned from the doctor today and found out I have colon cancer myself," he said, choking back tears.

I was stunned, not sure what to say next. I just managed to squeak out, "I'll pray for you."

A couple hours later, as I was preaching in the conference, my head was still spinning from the restaurant experience. When I finished speaking, I had a prayer team come up to minister to the sick. I stood on the platform and directed them. One man made his way around the prayer team and motioned for me to come down off the stage so he could talk to me. I reluctantly bent down to listen to his request.

"I was just diagnosed with colon cancer," he said. "I need you personally to pray for me!"

I have no idea what happened in the meeting after that. I was swimming in terror. I flew home from the conference a couple days later, my symptoms seemingly worsening by the hour. I was obsessed with my circumstances, and I still had a week to wait before my colonoscopy! I limped through the week, fighting off the images of death that continually plagued my mind. I was in our church the day before my test. Bill was preaching that morning, and when he concluded his message, he asked for the prayer team to come up to minister to those who needed a miracle in their bodies. I thought it would be good to pray for other people just to get my mind off of my own problems. About fifty people were on the ministry team that morning, and a couple hundred sick people lined up for prayer.

I was relieved to see only four folks in my prayer line. The first man came up, and I leaned over and whispered in his ear, "What do you need prayer for?"

"I have colon cancer," he said, with tears streaming down his cheeks. "I need God to heal me."

By now you probably have guessed what the other three wanted prayer for—colon cancer! Every one of them! Yikes!

Later that day, a young man who had been healed from colitis prayed for me. I did not really feel anything happen when he ministered to me, but all my symptoms left. The next morning I went to the specialist for the colonoscopy. He did not find *anything* wrong with me. It has been many years since that experience, and my symptoms have never returned!

In the previous chapters, we talked about the schemes of the enemy. Until I went through the trial with my colon issue, I never realized how complex his devices could be. It is so important that we keep ourselves prepared for action so that we do not fall prey to deceptive mind games that can war against our souls. We have to remind ourselves that we are Kingdom people destined to live in righteousness, peace and joy. We continually must cultivate the garden of our hearts by feeding the soil of our minds with truth. We must refuse to believe lies about ourselves that sow weed seed into our beings, seeds that destroy our confidence and undermine our destiny. And finally, we must water the orchard of our hearts with words that build, edify and comfort us, realizing that we are the beloved of God.

7

Serious Joy

Christians should be the happiest people on the planet!
Think about it—Jesus prayed, "I come to You [Father];
and these things I speak in the world so that they may have
My joy made full in themselves" (John 17:13). Jesus wants us
to be full of His joy! Hebrews 1:9 says that Jesus was anointed
with joy beyond His companions. This means He was happier
than the people He hung out with. Now that is a lot of *joy*! To
make us even happier, God sent His Holy Spirit into our lives to
comfort us. It is amazing that He wants us to be comfortable.
But wait, it gets even better. The Bible says that the fruit or
evidence of the Holy Spirit working in us is "love, joy, peace,
patience, kindness, goodness, faithfulness, gentleness, self-
control" (Galatians 5:22–23). There is that *joy* word again. We
have both the joy of Jesus and the joy of the Holy Spirit. Did
you get that? We have been given a double anointing for joy!

Now if that does not get you excited, then how about
this: "The kingdom of God is not eating and drinking, but

righteousness and peace and joy in the Holy Spirit" (Romans 14:17). Wow, one third of the Kingdom is joy! The apostle Peter said that we should "greatly rejoice with joy inexpressible and full of glory" (1 Peter 1:8). But joy is a foreign emotion for many Christians because religious spirits have deviously crept into their souls and have stolen the abundant life Jesus purchased for them.

The Power of Laughter

What cannot be expressed in words is often manifested in laughter. It is really hard to be extremely joyful and not laugh! People have always known that laughter—good, honest belly laughter, not the mocking kind—makes you feel better. Solomon said it thousands of years ago: "A joyful heart is good medicine" (Proverbs 17:22). Yet modern medicine has only been seriously studying the specific benefits of laughter for about thirty years.

Norman Cousins is most often credited for putting the healing power of laughter on the map scientifically. Cousins was a political journalist and activist who, after a grueling trip to Russia, developed ankylosing spondylitis, a form of arthritis in the spine. Nearly immobilized by pain, he was informed by his doctor that only one person in five hundred ever recovered from this condition. Hearing this, Cousins decided to take matters into his own hands. With the help of one of his doctors, he devised an unorthodox treatment plan. He moved out of the hospital into a hotel room, quit taking pain medication, started taking high doses of vitamin C and spent hours watching old Marx Brothers movies and *Candid Camera* spoofs in order to inspire laughter.

"It worked," recorded Cousins in his book *Anatomy of an Illness*. "I made the joyous discovery that ten minutes of genuine belly laughter had an anesthetic effect and would give me at least two hours of pain-free sleep."[1] After only a few weeks of this "treatment," Cousins's pain had diminished enough to allow him to return to work, and he went on to make a full recovery.

Scientists now have several theories about why laughter relieves pain. They think that it releases endorphins, relaxes our muscles or perhaps simply distracts us. They all agree, however, that Norman Cousins was not a special case. Laughter is definitely a painkiller! They have also been discovering that laughter does a whole host of other good things for our bodies, minds, emotions and relationships.

The physical act of laughter helps our bodies in three basic ways. First, it essentially does the same thing as a workout—it gets our lungs breathing more deeply, our hearts pumping faster and many of our muscles engaged, thereby improving our circulation and blood pressure. Second, it relaxes our bodies and stops our brains from producing stress hormones that suppress our immune systems, wear us down and make us vulnerable to disease. In 2005, doctors at the University of Maryland Medical Center declared that laughter is some of the "best medicine" for protecting us from America's leading cause of death, heart disease, because it prevents stress from deteriorating the lining of our blood vessels.[2] Third, laughter activates our immune systems. Studies have shown that laughter increases our natural defenses against cancer, viruses and upper-respiratory problems.[3]

Laughter and humor are also vital tools for creating and sustaining mental and emotional health, which, of course, directly affect our physical health. The many stresses we experience produce negative emotions like fear, grief and anger. Unless those are processed through cathartic releases like laughing, crying or yelling, they make us toxic in body and mind. The increasing number of mental health professionals in the "laughter therapy" movement argue that laughter on the physical level not only stops harmful stress hormones, it also stimulates helpful disease-fighting agents. On the emotional and mental levels, laughter not only diffuses negative thoughts and emotions, it also produces positive emotions like hope and elation and allows us to create new, more optimistic perspectives on our circumstances.

Concentration camp survivor Viktor Frankl saw firsthand that humor was a powerful survival skill that enabled him and other prisoners to hold on to hope and meaning through the darkest time of their lives. Frankl said, "Humor, more than anything else in the human makeup, affords an aloofness and an ability to rise above any situation, even if only for a few seconds."[4] Laughter researchers have now uncovered countless stories of people like Cousins and Frankl who have used humor to survive POW camps, cancer, war and other terrible losses, traumas and illnesses, as well as the daily grind at stressful jobs.

It is counterintuitive to laugh when life seems anything but funny. But according to proponents of therapeutic laughter, that is precisely the time to laugh, for the real power of laughter is not seen in funny circumstances, but in difficult ones. Laughter therapy is basically designed to teach people how to use laughter to move in the "opposite spirit" to their circumstances. In doing so, laughter becomes far more than an instinctive reaction. It becomes a skill by which people can cope with stress and stay healthy—a skill that happens, by the way, to be a key component of emotional intelligence. Research presents two facts that are helpful in developing this skill of laughter. First, contrary to what you might think, humor is not the number-one cause of laughter. Robert Provine, who has spent hundreds of hours studying people laughing throughout daily life, claims that laughter is primarily a social phenomenon, a universal human language—he actually calls it "speaking in tongues"—that facilitates social interaction and so shows up most in social settings.[5] On the one hand, this means that being with people is one of the best ways to develop the skill of laughter. On the other hand, it means that people who laugh more are naturally attractive to others and tend to develop stronger social networks, which are another important element in managing stress.

Research fact number two is this: The surest way to end up in a fit of hysterical laughter is to start by faking it. One of the leading figures in the secular laughter therapy movement, Dr. Madan Kataria, started a "laughter club" in his native India to see if he could reproduce the results Norman Cousins got from laughing. After the group ran out of funny jokes to tell, Kataria discovered that laughing "for no reason" worked just as well.[6] The physical act of laughter, even when forced initially, produces the same good physical, emotional and mental effects that can be inspired by humor or social cues, and these real effects in turn cause the laughter to become genuine.

I realize that Dr. Kataria is known as "the founder of the laughter yoga movement" and that many Christians find in yoga disturbing elements of Eastern religions and the demonic (as I do). I am not advocating the practice of yoga;

I am simply pointing out that even those in the world now recognize the therapeutic benefits of laughter. Look at the secular results alone. Kataria's discovery, on which he has developed the whole system of laughter exercises he calls "laughter yoga," has set off a chain reaction—his laughter clubs have multiplied and spread across the globe like wildfire. He has been featured on *Oprah* and written up in the *New Yorker*, *Time* and *Forbes*. His website overflows with testimonials of people claiming that laughter has restored joy in their lives, helped them cope with chronic pain and illness, healed and strengthened strained relationships and otherwise transformed their lives. Many even say they believe laughter yoga is the key to world peace! Videos on the site display laughter club participants dancing and playing around, all the while laughing uproariously. At moments they almost look as if they are in a revival meeting.

What all of this tells me is that the world is being primed to recognize the power and value of joy in their lives. Dr. Kataria's laughter yoga represents the best natural man can achieve in secular society with the God-given gift of laughter. Can you imagine what it will be like when the supernatural version infused with God's power hits the same tipping point of publicity? Religious people will probably still be getting their tails in a knot over what we call holy laughter, which I will talk more about in a minute, but the world will be ready to receive it because secular people already understand the value of laughing "for no reason." When the Body of Christ finally shows them the greatest reason to laugh—actually imparts to them the joy of the Creator—I am sure they will not even hesitate to join the party.

Holy Laughter

Speaking of parties, in 1994 God supernaturally fell on a small church in Toronto, Canada. One of the main manifestations of the Spirit's presence in what became known as the "Toronto Blessing" was "holy laughter." Much of the religious world rejected the movement, branding it as ridiculous, unbiblical and/or heretical.

It is not hard to understand why some people rejected the manifestations of this movement. At first glance, people literally falling down and rolling on the floor while laughing hysterically for no apparent reason can seem mindless and purposeless. But reports began to emerge from the Toronto Airport Vineyard Church of people being healed and restored from the inside out. Such reports overcame the ridiculous appearance of the manifestations of God. This resulted in millions of people flocking to the church from all over the world!

I have personally witnessed thousands of people being overcome by the invisible presence of the Holy Spirit. This movement has dramatically touched my wife, Kathy, who is a very emotionally stable person. There are seasons where she is so overcome by God's presence that she behaves as if she were completely intoxicated. Watching Kathy act so silly was troubling at first, but I have seen that the fruit of these experiences has been overwhelmingly positive in both her life and in the lives of many others. This has caused me to hunger for the same experience myself.

Long before I read anything on what scientists were learning in their experiments with laughter, God was already causing His people to laugh their way into wholeness. While many sneered and mocked, millions of people

117

were becoming whole. I guess Solomon had it right thousands of years ago when he wrote, "A merry heart doeth good like a medicine" (Proverbs 17:22, KJV). Maybe it is time for the Church of the living God to become a pharmacy!

The Armor of God

It is A.D. 62, and the Romans have imprisoned the apostle Paul again. The scene is grim; with no ventilation or fresh air in his cell, the prison is hot and unbearably humid. The stench of human waste impregnates the atmosphere. The weight of iron shackles that cusp Paul's hands and feet fatigue the frail body of this old man. Tight security prohibits blades, resulting in the prisoner's hair and beard growing unkempt and matted. Darkness prevails in the windowless cell, yet eventually, Paul's eyes adjust enough to painfully eke out four letters that will later be called the "Prison Epistles."

There is little visitation in this seemingly godforsaken rat hole, except for the intimidating presence of the Roman guards who ruthlessly peer into the cells to check on the prisoners. In a strange way, these adversarial sentinels become a welcome contrast in the prisoners' lives as these lonely souls wrestle with their fate while awaiting their sentencing from the merciless Roman magistrates.

It was here that the great apostle Paul forged his letter to the Ephesians. In stunning contrast to his impoverished condition, he wrote:

> Paul, an apostle of Christ Jesus by the will of God, to the saints who are at Ephesus and who are faithful in Christ Jesus: Grace to you and peace from God our Father and the Lord Jesus Christ. Blessed be the God and Father of our Lord Jesus Christ, who has blessed us with every spiritual blessing in the heavenly places in Christ, just as He chose us in Him before the foundation of the world, that we would be holy and blameless before Him.
>
> Ephesians 1:1–4

His message is clear: You can imprison my body, shackle my members and restrict my visitation, but you cannot incarcerate my joy, fetter my blessing or steal my inheritance. Many people, living in cozy twenty-first-century comfort that was foreign to kings just a hundred years ago, complain of their tough situations. They fail to recognize that their coming heavenly seat supersedes their earthly circumstances (see Ephesians 2:6).

I have a very wealthy friend who, many years ago, was going through an incredibly tough situation. His marriage was on the rocks, his relationship with his only son was strained and his business was in serious financial trouble. He became so depressed over his circumstances that for the first time in his life, he decided to see a professional counselor. After much research, he flew halfway across the country in his own private plane to see one of the most highly esteemed psychologists in America.

When he sat down in the doctor's office, the counselor asked him, "So why have you come to see me?"

"My marriage is struggling, my relationship with my son is bad and my business is failing. My circumstances are depressing me," my friend responded.

"No, happiness is an inside job!" the psychologist countered.

To the psychologist's shock, my friend stood up, walked over to his desk and wrote out a check for $300. The doctor said, "What are you doing? You've only been here for five minutes."

"Well, I got what I came for," he responded. "I thought that my circumstances were dictating my depression. Now I understand that my situation does not determine my inner condition. I realize now that the kingdom around me does not have power over the Kingdom within me. Thank you for your help, doctor," my friend explained as he exited the building. He flew home with a brand-new attitude, although his external circumstances would go unchanged for nearly two more years.

Many people's circumstances dictate their stances. They become powerless victims of other people's actions and attitudes. They wrongly believe that their physical situation *is* their condition. The truth is, you do not always have power over what happens to you, but you do have complete control over what happens in you.

Seated in Heavenly Places

In Ephesians, Paul depicts three distinct seasons in our lives. He uses the posture of *sitting, walking* and *standing* metaphorically to represent these seasons. In the early days of his imprisonment, Paul wrote,

> God, being rich in mercy, because of His great love with which
> He loved us, even when we were dead in our transgressions,

121

made us alive together with Christ (by grace you have been saved), and raised us up with Him, and *seated us with Him in the heavenly places in Christ Jesus*, so that in the ages to come He might show the surpassing riches of His grace in kindness toward us in Christ Jesus.

Ephesians 2:4–7, emphasis added

I love the "relax, kick back and sip some suds" seasons of our lives. The Son of God experienced these kinds of seasons Himself. Remember when the Father said to Him, "Sit at my right hand until I make your enemies a footstool for your feet" (Psalm 110:1)? Times like these remind me of David's words in Psalm 23:2–3: "He makes me lie down in green pastures; He leads me beside quiet waters. He restores my soul." I want to say to God, "*O Lord, please make me lie down in those green pastures . . . kill me with Your kindness . . . cuddle me with Your comfort . . . lavish me in Your luxury . . . whisper to me Your sweet nothings and kiss me into new dimensions of Your love.*"

It is in these wonderful times in life that God teaches us about His love, mercy and grace. I call these seasons *"It's all about God"* seasons. In these times, it seems that if I make any great efforts like trying to work hard, pray long or study diligently, that kind of messes it up. I know these are times that I am supposed to learn how to rest in God and how to trust Him with my entire life, but it almost feels as though God is sanctioning "lazy."

Let me be clear here—I know laziness is not an admirable quality in the Kingdom. I am just trying to describe how it *feels* when we are in a season of rest. In these times, phrases that include words like warfare, weapons, struggle or battle seem irrelevant. It is like relaxing in a hot tub while reading a murder mystery. We are so far from the battlefield that it feels fictional rather than factual.

Many believers never experience springtime in God. It is almost as if these folks were born in the Antarctic spiritually speaking, where it is always cold and there is no spring. I have found a common denominator among most of these Frozen Chosen. For them, "being seated in heavenly places" is a poetic metaphor, an intellectual philosophy or a theological wish rather than a radical reality. It is only when we learn to live from the inside out, and not from the outside in, that we are truly free to experience these seasons. The Kingdom within us is more powerful than the kingdom around us.

As I explained in great detail in my book *Heavy Rain: How You Can Transform the World Around You*,[1] we have dual citizenship. We are citizens of heaven and citizens of earth. The question is, do we live from earth toward heaven or do we live from heaven toward earth? When our heavenly seat is just a distant promise, we live in defense mode all the time. We are always praying about something that has already happened. Prayers like "O God, heal my friend," or "O God, fix my finances," or "O God, help reconcile my relationship" are all defensive prayers.

The hard circumstances of our existence provoke these supplications, and it is important that we pray about anything that has gone wrong in the world around us. But when our entire prayer life is motivated by the negative circumstances surrounding us, it is a symptom of our seating arrangement. Earthly seating creates reactionary prayers. If we sit there long enough, we will wind up with a big devil and a little God.

On the other hand, when we take our rightful place seated with Christ on His heavenly throne, we live powerfully, offensively and relatively peacefully. Our prayers become prophetic declarations that direct history. The Kingdom within us begins to direct the world around us so that we're no longer victims, but victors! It is in these "seated," all-about-God seasons that we learn how to live out this radical reality.

Walking in the High Call of God

I envision the aged apostle Paul persevering through the long, perilous nights in that dark, damp dungeon. He struggles to his feet, his body etched from beatings and stoning. Racked with pain, the old man begins to pace the floor of his cell as he meticulously inscribes this phrase on parchment: "Therefore I, the prisoner of the Lord, implore you to *walk* in a manner worthy of the calling with which you have been called" (Ephesians 4:1, emphasis added).

Could it be that the great apostle, with his body stiff and weary but his mind enlightened, recalls the words of the prophet Habakkuk? "The Lord GOD is my strength, and He has made my feet like hinds' feet, and makes me walk on high places" (Habakkuk 3:19). Or maybe the old saint is simply inspired by the shifting wind of the Holy Spirit as he senses the season changing. Whatever God used to stir these *walking* words in Paul, they stand in sharp contrast to the *seated* expressions that he penned just days earlier.

Walking seasons are marked by our initiatives to co-labor with God's divine purposes, to extend the borders of the Kingdom into the lives of others. As the winds of change blow over our lives, the elements inspire different attributes of

The Armor of God

God to emerge from our personhood. The time to sit resting in His grace has passed, and now it is time for His power to flow through our efforts as we walk out His high call in our lives. When we understand the spiritual seasons of our lives, then we can raise our sails and let His wind drive us to the shores of destiny. But when we are seated when we should be walking, it undermines His ways and derails His purposes.

Moses experienced this shifting wind in the book of Exodus. He recorded it like this:

> Moses said to the people, "Do not fear! Stand by and see the salvation of the LORD which He will accomplish for you today; for the Egyptians whom you have seen today, you will never see them again forever. The LORD will fight for you while you keep silent."
>
> Then the LORD said to Moses, "Why are you crying out to Me? Tell the sons of Israel to go forward."
>
> Exodus 14:13–15

Did you catch what is going on here? Moses told the people to *stand* and watch God work miraculously. But, in essence, God said to Moses, *Stop your whining and start walking!* There are times in our lives where God simply refuses to do anything for us unless He does it with us! There we are, lying down in green pastures . . . still waters soothing our souls . . . and God says, *What are you doing? Get up and start walking through the valley!*

I often want to say, "Hey, God, You're the one who made me lie down here. You're the one who said to sit here while You make my enemies a footstool for my feet. What's up with this new attitude?" Yet in many ways, the walking seasons are the most exciting times. Powerful things happen when God is working through us to destroy the works of the devil. All sorts of victories usually mark walking seasons—people are healed as we lay hands on them, miraculous provision takes place as we sow our bag lunch into His field, marriages are reconciled through a few wise words that may seem insignificant. Victory is in the air, and hope fills our hearts.

Standing in the Presence of Our Enemies

Weeks had passed since the great apostle Paul had begun his letter to the saints of Ephesus. The grueling task had taken its toll on the elder statesman as he persistently pushed past his circumstances in the Roman prison to pen his timeless epistle.

The apostles seemed to have a knack for prison breaks. Around A.D. 44, Peter was supernaturally released from a high-security prison in Jerusalem, which resulted in King Herod ordering the execution of all the guards (see Acts 12:5–19). Paul and Silas were also famous for their jailbreaks. Years earlier, the apostles were worshiping in a Roman dungeon when suddenly an earthquake rocked the prison's foundations. The penitentiary doors burst open, and all the prisoners' stocks fell off. Paul mercifully refused to leave the prison so the life of the guards would be spared (see Acts 16:25–30).

This time, the Romans were taking no chances with their notorious prisoner. The king ordered a regiment of his fiercest, best-equipped and most loyal soldiers to guard Paul's cell. Even though the prisoners were behind iron bars, locked in shackles and in a stone-reinforced penitentiary, every guard was fully prepared to thwart any kind of escape plan.

One day as Paul peered through the entrapment of his cell, his eyes were drawn to the soldiers' equipment. As he surveyed the guards' weapons and armor, he evaluated their distinct purposes and the Holy Spirit began to speak to him:

> Finally, be strong in the Lord and in the strength of His might. Put on the full armor of God, so that you will be able to *stand* firm against the schemes of the devil. For our struggle is not against flesh and blood, but against the rulers, against the powers, against the world forces of this darkness, against the spiritual forces of wickedness in the heavenly places. Therefore, take up the full armor of God, so that you will be able to resist in the evil day, and having done everything, *to stand firm. Stand firm* therefore, HAVING GIRDED YOUR LOINS WITH TRUTH, and HAVING PUT ON THE BREASTPLATE OF RIGHTEOUSNESS, and HAVING SHOD YOUR FEET WITH THE PREPARATION OF THE GOSPEL OF PEACE; in addition to all, taking up the shield of faith with which you will be able to extinguish all the flaming arrows of the evil one. And take THE HELMET OF SALVATION, and the sword of the Spirit, which is the word of God. With all prayer and petition pray at all times in the Spirit, and with this in view, be on the alert with all perseverance and petition for all the saints.
>
> Ephesians 6:10–18, emphasis added

Before we step back into the prison and evaluate the armor of the Roman guards, I want you to notice something profound. Weeks had passed since the apostle Paul had begun this book we now call Ephesians, and the spiritual season had changed again. Paul is no longer talking to us about sitting in heavenly places, nor is he encouraging us to walk out our high call. Instead, we find him exhorting us to stand firm! He says that when we have done everything to stand, then we just need to *stand*. These words represent the perilous times when the goal of our Christian existence is to hold our ground, not take more territory. These are days of warfare, when the facts look like fiction and we wish this were just a novel instead of our life.

I can only imagine that as the prisoner penned the final paragraphs of what I believe is one of the most insightful books of his life, the demonic resistance in the prison cell must have dramatically increased. An intense struggle probably ensued as principalities and powers wrestled against Paul's very soul. The final verses that conclude this great epistle stand in stark contrast to the victorious words that framed his initial thoughts just weeks earlier.

In six short chapters, Paul has transitioned us from sitting with Christ on His throne while using the enemy as a footstool to a no-holds-barred wrestling match with demonic spirits trying to wreak havoc on our lives. I think a couple of paradoxical passages concerning Christ's ministry demonstrate the *feel* of these contrasting spiritual seasons. Luke records a powerful time:

> One day He was teaching; and there were some Pharisees and teachers of the law sitting there, who had come from every village of Galilee and Judea and from Jerusalem; *and the power of the Lord was present for Him to perform healing.*
>
> Luke 5:17, emphasis added

Yet Matthew recounts a nearly powerless time that happened when Jesus was teaching in His hometown (kind of funny that His worst day was still better than most of our best days): "They took offense at Him. . . . *And He did not do many miracles there* because of their unbelief" (Matthew 13:57–58, emphasis added).

I think you get the point. Even Jesus experienced different spiritual seasons in His life and ministry. I love the "seated" seasons, and I enjoy taking a good, long "walk" down destiny lane in the fruit-bearing seasons, but I cannot say that I have ever enjoyed the wrestling match of the "standing" seasons!

Insights from the Armor

We have spent a lot of time describing spiritual warfare in the pages of this book. Now let's go back to Paul's cell and see what insights we can gain through his revelation in Ephesians 6 about the Roman soldiers' battle gear.

1) **Gird Your Loins with Truth:** Every Roman soldier wore a wide, sturdy belt that he put on before any of his other armor. The belt supported his abdominal muscles and helped protect his midsection.

Spiritual ramifications: The word for *truth* in this passage does not refer to the Bible, although the essence of all truth is the Word of God. This word *truth* means "real." Many people hide behind a façade, never really allowing others to get to know them. Like Adam and Eve covering themselves with fig leaves to hide their shame, many believers dress themselves in man-made realities that are easily penetrated by demonic spirits. Although they may be able to fool some people with their veneer personality, in times of intense battle their lack of depth will expose them to the elements. Paul therefore exhorts us to be honest, live with integrity and be real with God and with people He has placed in our lives. Dishonesty is an open door that will wreak havoc in our lives, especially during any kind of enemy siege.

2) **The Breastplate of Righteousness:** The breastplate covered a soldier's heart and other vital organs.

Spiritual ramifications: Thousands of years ago the wisest man in the world wrote, "Watch over your heart with all diligence, for from it flow the springs of life" (Proverbs 4:23). Our heart is the seat of our soul and the footstool of our spirit. When we received Christ, we underwent heart transplant surgery. Jesus Christ was the willing donor. We do not produce righteousness; we protect it. Righteousness is a part of our new nature that we received as a gift (see Romans 5:17). The enemy would love to convince us that our heart is wicked and our ways are evil, but the devil is a lying accuser. The righteousness of God is the breastplate of every Christian's life. No worries, He's got you covered!

3) **The Sandals of Peace:** The sandals Roman soldiers wore had cleats on the bottom like some of today's athletic shoes. This provided stability in combat. I call them "cleats of peace."

Spiritual ramifications: These cleats of peace help us in times of war to stay connected to our *under*-standing (foundation) of love. It is interesting that when Paul wrote to the Romans, he said, "The God of peace will soon crush Satan under your feet" (Romans 16:20). When we love those who hate us and pray for those who persecute us, we extend the Gospel of peace to a godless and destructive world. Humanity is the devil's enemy; he has no friends on this planet. He works hard to get people to destroy one another. Jesus said, "Do not resist an evil person; but whoever slaps you on your right cheek, turn the other to him also" (Matthew 5:39). The Lord is not promoting a passive gospel—just ask the money changers in the Temple. But Jesus is teaching us how to transform evil ecosystems. For example, if somebody punches me and I automatically punch them back, then I am reacting and the people around me are externally controlling my actions. But if somebody whacks me and I respond by not hitting them back, instead of reacting, I break the ecosystem of evil and extend the Gospel of peace. I prove there is a force within me that is stronger than the force around me. And finally, I let the devil know that flesh and blood is not my enemy, which ultimately defeats his devious purposes.

When I came on staff at Bethel Church in 1998, several witches attended our services. One of the main witches from the local coven was recently saved in our church, so the people from the coven came to church to mess with their ex-leader by trying to disrupt our services. They would throw curses at us while we were preaching. Our prayer warriors would battle back by breaking the curses and rebuking the witches. The whole thing went on for more than a year. At times it got a little hairy. The main problem was that our congregation was pretty frightened by our new friends, and they lost their peace. Of course, when you lose your peace, you lose your footing and faith gives way to fear. After several months of this chaotic warfare, I had had enough. I decided to enact a new strategy. Whenever I discerned that witches were present in our assembly, I would leave my seat and work my way over to where they were sitting. Then I would give each of them a big hug and tell them how much I loved them. They did not quite know what to do with a hug and a little love. It freaked them out. They were really fortified against rebukes and curses, but they had no defense for love. Over the next year or so, several of them received Christ, and the rest of them finally stopped coming to church. Love never fails.

4) **The Shield of Faith:** A Roman shield was constructed with a wooden frame and covered by a thick layer of leather. Often the leather was soaked with water to make it fireproof (to extinguish the flaming arrows of the enemy). The shield was three or four feet tall and two feet wide. This made it large enough that a soldier could crouch down behind it and protect his entire body. A regiment of soldiers could overlap their shields and create a wall of fortification from their enemies.

Spiritual ramifications: We are called "believers" for a reason. Ultimately, the real war is waged on the battlefield of faith. The simple but profound question is, Whom will we believe? Will we believe the enemy's accusations? Will we believe our circumstances, our well-meaning friends, or will we believe God? Thirty-eight times in the New Testament alone, the phrase "the faith" is used to describe our walk with God. Make no mistake about it; the demonic realm is out to steal our faith! The infamous serpent in the Garden began his devious plot to undermine the destiny of mankind with the words, "Indeed, has God said . . . ?" (Genesis 3:1). The names have changed, but the strategy is as old as Adam and Eve: to cause people to question God's promises in their lives. Do whatever is necessary—undermine, twist, challenge, question, dilute, emasculate, weaken, pollute, contaminate, infect, dispute or disrupt the Word of God in the hearts of people. But when we humble ourselves behind our shields of faith and refuse to believe anything that is contrary to the Word of God and the promises of God in our lives, we extinguish the flaming arrows of the evil one. The plot is exposed; his scheme is destroyed and the victory is assured by faith!

5) **The Helmet of Salvation:** The Romans had a couple of different kinds of helmets. One was made of leather with metal plates sewn to it. Another type was cast from one solid piece of metal in the shape of the warrior's head. There is a great story of a Roman soldier named Brutus Maximus, who fought a violent battle with his entire face covered with a mask of steel. He did not cast the mask in his own image; instead, he molded it in the image of his emperor, Caesar Augustus. Wearing it not only protected his face and eyes, but said to his enemies, "I see you through my emperor's eyes. I represent him on this battlefield. I am fighting for his glory."

Spiritual ramifications: Crazy things can happen in the heat of battle, as we observed in the book of Nehemiah. The enemy will do whatever it takes to steal our confidence and undermine our relationship with God. But a head covered with the helmet of salvation will rest by the still waters of a Kingdom mentality. Paul said it best: "The peace of God, which surpasses all understanding, will guard your hearts and your minds through Christ Jesus" (Philippians 4:7). The prophet Isaiah put it this way: "You will keep him in perfect peace, whose mind is stayed on You" (Isaiah 26:3, NKJV). The quickest way to lose our peace in the midst of a spiritual conflict is to forget that our salvation came from His works and not ours. If our salvation was won through our efforts, then it would be up to us to fight to keep it. But we are not fighting *for* our salvation—we are fighting *from* our salvation. Our helmet should be molded from these one-piece, titanium verses: "For by grace you have been saved through faith, and that not of yourselves; it is the gift of God; not as a result of works, so that no one may boast" (Ephesians 2:8–9).

I cannot tell you how many times people have come up and told me that they no longer feel saved. Salvation is not a feeling any more than being human is a feeling. Can you imagine someone going to a doctor and saying, "Doc, I just don't feel human anymore"?

"Well, Johnny," the physician might respond, "do you feel like a dog? Maybe you've become a dog!"

This is ridiculous, of course. But many Christians base their relationship with God on their feelings, which is also ridiculous. The devil plays on these emotional mindsets, putting us on the endless merry-go-round of insecurity. We must exit this merry-go-round with self-confidence or we will remain dizzy and disoriented. Our confidence must be rooted in God's ability to redeem us, not in our ability to save ourselves.

6) **The Sword of the Spirit:** The Roman sword was actually an eighteen-inch-long knife, razor sharp on both edges. It was used in hand-to-hand combat.

Spiritual ramifications: The "Word of God," which is the sword of the Spirit, does not specifically refer to the Bible in this passage. The Greek word here for "Word of God" is *rhema*, which most Greek scholars render as "God-breathed." If Paul were simply talking about the Bible being the sword of the Spirit, he would have more accurately used the Greek word *logos*. I would like to suggest that the Word of God that we use to judge the thoughts and intentions of our own hearts is a different sword than the one we use to defend ourselves against demonic assaults. Maybe it would be clearer to read

Ephesians 6:17 as "Take the helmet of salvation, and the sword of the Spirit, which is the *rhema* of God," and to read Hebrews 4:12 as "For the *logos* of God is living and active and sharper than any two-edged sword, and piercing as far as the division of soul and spirit, of both joints and marrow, and able to judge the thoughts and intentions of the heart."

The writer of Hebrews makes it clear that the Bible is the standard by which all thoughts and intentions of the heart should be judged, but Paul is making a different point in Ephesians. He is telling us that listening to the Holy Spirit and prophetically proclaiming what He says is our only offensive weapon of warfare. We covered this earlier in the book, when we looked at Paul's exhortation to Timothy to take the prophecies that were previously spoken over him, and with them, fight the good fight (see 1 Timothy 1:18).

The sword of the Spirit, however, cannot be confined to just prophetic declarations. It would also include anything God breathes on when we are in a wrestling match with demonic powers. For example, God often breathes on the *logos* and makes it *rhema* in the midst of our greatest battles. The most important thing to remember here is that it is the Spirit's sword being wielded. All our offensive firepower is vested in the Holy Spirit. He protects us, comforts us, teaches us and leads us into all truth. When all hell breaks loose in our lives, we must stay close to heaven by cultivating a relationship with God's Spirit.

9

Casting Out Demons

His name was Henry, and he was our cleanup boy at the repair shop I managed in Weaverville, California. Henry was about sixteen when I first met him. Being raised in the woods had made him kind of a country bumpkin. He was lanky and stood about five-foot-eight, with mangy blond hair. He talked constantly. Henry did not really need anything to talk about, he just liked to talk. And Henry definitely was not the sharpest knife in the drawer. For example, one day the UPS driver had left several packages on my workbench. I opened them and removed all the parts from the packaging. About half an hour later, Henry walked in and started talking, as usual. I was lying on a creeper underneath a car and was hardly paying attention to him, but every once in a while I would give him a courtesy, "Uh-huh . . . yup . . . I see your point . . . you're right about that . . . sure."

Suddenly, something Henry said caught my attention. "Where'd you get these boxes of puffcorn?" he asked. "This stuff has no taste at all!"

I rolled out from under the car in time to see Henry eating the Styrofoam packing peanuts from the shipping boxes. Needless to say, I did not see Henry for at least a week. His dad said something about him having the flu.

About a year after I met Henry, I led him to Christ—or at least I think I did. But his antics continued for years—five car wrecks, several arrests for public intoxication, breaking this and crashing that . . . it never ended. Yet the more I got to know Henry, the better I understood his behavior. His father had molested him from the time he was a little boy, deep into his teen years. His mother pretended not to know. His older brother was a violent alcoholic who pounded on him on a regular basis. His sister . . . well, let's just say that she was Henry's clone. The entire clan reminded me of the Addams family. I was doing my best to disciple Henry, but I had never met anybody so messed up in all my life. He had homosexual tendencies and alcohol, drug and porn addictions. And to make matters worse, he would have fits of rage where he would scream obscenities at God in the middle of the church parking lot. I was young and ignorant, and I did not really know what to do with him.

Then one day Henry came into the Union 76 station I had recently purchased. It was a busy summer day, and we were swamped with work. Of course, Henry made his way to the back of the shop where I was working on a car.

"I need you . . . I need . . . I need you to pray for me!" he begged. "Something is inside of me and it's trying to kill me!"

"Henry, I can't talk to you right now! I'm up to my neck in alligators. You need to get out of here," I insisted.

"Please, just a quick prayer . . . . all I need is a quick prayer," he moaned.

"All right, Henry—thirty seconds, that's all I'm giving you—thirty seconds," I said, obviously irritated. "Step into the storage room and I'll pray for you."

My goal was just to give him a quick *"I release peace over you in Jesus' name"* prayer. We stepped into the tiny storage room the size of a small walk-in closet. Henry bowed his head, and I put my hand on his chest and began to pray.

Before I could get to "in Jesus' name," Henry grabbed me by the throat and started choking me, screaming in a strange voice, *"I've come to kill you. . . . I've come to destroy you!"*

I shouted back, *"I rebuke you in the name of Jesus! I plead the blood of Jesus over you! In Jesus' name, you murdering spirit, be gone!"*

Nothing seemed to work. If anything, Henry got more violent. He was shaking, choking, biting and scratching me. At one point, he grabbed my new uniform shirt and ripped it almost entirely off my body.

Gasping for air, I decided to change my strategy by choking him back! I wrestled with Henry for several minutes, trying desperately to free myself from his grip. We slammed into the shelving units that lined the two opposing walls. They were stocked to the ceiling with automotive filters. The shelves collapsed on us like dominos, leaving us wrestling underneath a large pile of air and oil filters. I continued shouting rebukes as I struggled to free myself from Henry's choke hold.

Suddenly, without warning, he let go of my neck, shoved the pile of debris aside and stood up. "They're gone!" he said with a sigh. "I feel free!"

Henry thanked me, got in his car and drove off . . . leaving me alone. There I was, face and hair covered in dirt, shirt ripped nearly in half, shoulders, face and chest badly scratched, with teeth marks on my hands. I looked like the final scene in a Rambo movie.

Unfortunately, Henry's newfound freedom would not last for long. This scene repeated itself over and over again in both our lives. My deliverance ministry looked a lot more like the seven sons of Sceva's than like any disciple of Christ's (see Acts 19:14–16). Over the next ten years, several more "Henrys" came into my life. There was the 32-year-old beauty queen who had to be held down by four strong men. When I demanded that they let her go so that I could "get her free," she sprung to her feet and kicked me in the chest, bruising the right side of my rib cage. It turns out she was the two-time women's karate champion of the world.

And then there was the gal who was running down the street buck naked. By the time I got to the house to help, they had her wrapped in a sheet and were restraining her. This time I was sure I had the mind of the Spirit. "Let her go!" I insisted.

"Kris," they protested, "she's naked and out of control!"

"No problem, I got it handled," I assured them. A second later she was running around the house, still with nothing on. "Restrain her!" I shouted. "Hold her down!"

For years, my deliverance ministry resembled scenes straight out of *The Exorcist*. (I actually never saw the movie. The movie trailer was more than I could handle.)

A long time ago, I was sharing the stories of my failed deliverances in a ministry school. After several crazy narratives, a young student could not take it any longer. He stood up and interrupted me, shouting, *"When I tell demons to leave, they leave! I'm a child of the King, and I don't put up with any of their antics."*

"That's awesome," I said, slightly sarcastically. "How many deliverances have you done?"

"Three," he said with confidence.

"Beginner's luck!" I teased.

Getting It Right

You would think that a guy who was once demonized would know how to get someone else free. The truth is that although I have been involved in hundreds of deliverances, in my first dozen years I rarely saw anyone get truly free. At times the demons would actually leave for a short season, but soon they would be back in full force. The small town of Weaverville provided a great laboratory in which believers could learn how people could stay free. With a population of about three thousand, the community was small enough that we lived in close proximity to the people whom we practiced deliverance on. This gave us a prime opportunity to observe whether or not people actually changed when they "got free."

So many crazy things are done in the name of deliverance that it is frightening. In my opinion, there are more people who need to get delivered from the trauma of their last deliverance than there are people who actually get delivered from demons. For example, I was in Australia recently when a man began to manifest demonically. Immediately, the elders rushed over with a large pail and tried to get the demonized man to "throw up" his evil spirits. In 2009, I was in a meeting in Holland when a demonized man began freaking out and throwing chairs. Several leaders gathered around him, screaming rebukes and pleading the blood of Jesus. A while back, a well-dressed middle-aged lady asked me if demons come out when you pour salt on a person. When I questioned her methods, she told me that her pastor, who was a prominent member of his denomination, taught his congregation that pouring salt on the head of a demonized person would free them from oppression.

I could fill an entire book with absurd stories of failed deliverances, many of which I led myself. Some of the stories are quite funny, but the sad thing is that those demonized people left unchanged, or worse yet, became traumatized from someone's efforts to get them free.

That leads me to the million-dollar question: How do people actually get free? And, just as important, how do they stay free?

Captives and Prisoners

I have learned over many years that the question about how people actually get free cannot be answered until we determine why they are bound. Isaiah said,

> The Spirit of the Lord GOD is upon me, because the LORD has anointed me to bring good news to the afflicted; He has sent me to bind up the brokenhearted, *to proclaim liberty to captives* and *freedom to prisoners.*
>
> Isaiah 61:1, emphasis added

Notice that the prophet is describing two kinds of people behind bars: *captives* and *prisoners*. Prisoners are criminals whom a judge sentences to jail. It takes a court order from the Judge to release spiritual prisoners. Captives are people who have been imprisoned through lies and deception. It takes knowledge of the Truth to set them free. When we are working to free someone who is demonized, we must first determine if the person is a captive or a prisoner.

Let's take a closer look at each of these and find out how both captives and prisoners can get free and stay free. We will begin by investigating the plight of the prisoners Jesus talks about in Matthew 18:21–35. Responding to Peter's question about how many times he ought to forgive, Jesus shared a story about our King and His Kingdom. He said that the Kingdom of heaven could be compared to a king who wished to settle accounts with his slaves. One slave owed the king what would be like a million dollars today. The slave begged for mercy, and the king forgave all that he owed. But that same slave went to his fellow slave, who owed him a small percentage relative to what he had owed the king, and demanded repayment immediately. When the guy asked for mercy, the first slave refused and had him thrown into prison.

When the king found out about it, he was extremely angry. He said, "You wicked slave, I forgave you all that debt because you pleaded with me. Should you not also have had mercy on your fellow slave, in the same way that I had mercy on you?" And moved with anger, he "handed him over to the torturers until he should repay all that was owed him." Likewise, Jesus said, "My heavenly Father will also do the same to you, if each of you does not forgive his brother from your heart" (verses 33–35).

It is clear from this story that God insists His people forgive one another. Many spend their lives hating others and planning revenge. But bitterness has no friends. It always leaks out onto those we love the most. When Christians refuse to forgive, God has a "ways and means committee" called the torturers who help drive bitterness and hatred out of our lives.

Unforgiveness imprisons our souls and opens the door to evil spirits in us. In my experience, unforgiveness is the number one reason why Christians are oppressed. In order for these prisoners to be set free, they must convince the Supreme Court Judge that they have forgiven those who have hurt and abused them. Forgiveness inspires a decree from the King, which in turn gives us authority to command these evil spirits to release their prisoner. Without a kingly decree, we may overpower the demonic spirits in a person's life and force them to leave temporarily, but they always return.

Demonic spirits are subject to the laws of God's Kingdom. They know full well when someone's lifestyle of sin has given them access to that person's soul. The power of the Spirit and the authority of Jesus Christ are required for someone to get free and stay free of demonic oppression. Trying to get a person delivered who refuses to forgive or who insists on holding onto a lifestyle of sin is a pointless waste of time.

Prisoners Freed

Not only do we need to forgive others, we *must* also forgive ourselves! This truth was driven home to me recently when I was ministering at a conference in Hawaii. After I finished my final session, two young girls came up to me for prayer. I could see the misery afflicting these young women. One of the girls was standing off to my side, waiting for her turn, while the other was clawing at herself as she stood in front of me. I began to pray for her. I quickly realized that this was not going to be one of those "*Jesus, come fill her up*" prayers. I was about to engage in a spiritual battle that I thought should be easily won, with all the authority we believers have been given in Christ.

As we began, she said, "I just want it to go away!"

"You want what to go away?" I asked.

"I want the punishment to go away! I can't stop punishing myself!" she cried.

I took her by the hands so she would not injure herself any further, and I began to look for the entry point of her pain. I could feel the Holy Spirit urging me to walk her through the process of loving herself, so I had her repeat after me, *"I love myself."*

At first, my words fell on hollow ears. She just trembled in front of me at the thought of repeating those words. A lot of time passed before she broke through the barrier of shame. She finally whispered, *"I love myself."*

We continued this process for a while, then I decided it was time to ask her why she was punishing herself. She explained that she had given herself away to a guy who she thought loved her. Shortly after that experience, he was gone and she was left alone with the shame of losing her innocence to a liar. The humiliation of losing her virginity deceitfully was more than she could take. The thought of what she had done plagued her like an incessant nightmare. The very thought of her ex-boyfriend sent her into a rage. Unable to escape the shame, she began to punish herself by having sex with several other men. Self-hatred and unforgiveness had become her closest friends. She was a powerless prisoner of her own demise.

I started her on the process of forgiving herself. Self-destructive roots had grown so deeply in her! I walked her through the theology of what Christ did for us on the cross

145

and how He became justice for us so that she could forgive herself. Then I had her ask Jesus how He sees the man who stole her virginity from her. (This question is a great tool for giving people compassion toward those whom they are struggling to forgive.) Jesus showed her that He loves the man, but grieves over him. She then was able to feel God's compassion for her ex-boyfriend and forgive him. Finally, she broke the partnership that she had made with the punisher as Jesus drove that spirit out of her.

Surprisingly, both girls that night had the same issue. Unforgiveness had enslaved their souls, and the punisher had become their prison guard. They had been bound by the regrets of the past, but they were freed that night and God restored them.

Demonized Christians?

My personal testimony in chapter 1 often inspires the question, Can a Christian be demon-possessed? The Greek word for "possessed," interestingly, is the word *echo*. In the context of demons it means "to have or hold possession of the mind or to be closely joined to a person or a thing." The Greek word *echo* is used in places like Luke 8:27:

> When He came out onto the land, He was met by a man from the city who was *possessed* [Greek word *echo*] with demons; and who had not put on any clothing for a long time, and was not living in a house, but in the tombs.

Of course, we get the sense that the person's thoughts, attitudes and behaviors were echoing the demonic spirit that had possessed him.

The New Testament contains two Greek words for "oppressed." One is the Greek word *thrauo*, which means "to break into pieces." Used to describe Jesus' ministry, the word appears in Luke 4:18:

> THE SPIRIT OF THE LORD IS UPON ME, BECAUSE HE HAS ANOINTED ME TO PREACH THE GOSPEL TO THE POOR. HE HAS SENT ME TO PROCLAIM RELEASE TO CAPTIVES, AND RECOVERY OF SIGHT TO THE BLIND, TO SET FREE THOSE WHO ARE OPPRESSED [Greek word *thrauo*].

The other word for "oppressed" in the Greek is *katadunasteuo*, which means, "to exercise power over someone." It is used in Acts 10:38:

> You know of Jesus of Nazareth, how God anointed Him with the Holy Spirit and with power, and how He went about doing good and healing all who were oppressed [Greek word *katadunasteuo*] by the devil, for God was with Him.

As Christians, we cannot be possessed in the sense that a demon would control our minds and actions, because when we receive Jesus, our bodies become the house of the Holy Spirit. In other words, we are already God's possession, so nothing else can take possession of us. Believers can, however, be oppressed by coming under the control of a demonic spirit and have their lives broken into pieces through a lifestyle of sin, as we talked about earlier.

I think it is important to mention here that when we talk about the spirit realm, our understanding tends to be limited to the natural laws of the visible world. We tend to explain spiritual realities with nice, neat definitions that fit our human vocabulary, even while arguing over the meaning of specific words in the original languages. This may help us to feel intelligent and well-informed, yet the spirit world will not stay in these well-defined boxes.

Anyone who has ever experienced the demonic realm or the angelic realm will tell you that our vocabulary is insufficient to describe the realities of this dimension. For example, we have principles like the laws of physics that make our world somewhat predictable. If somebody jumps off the roof of a house, the law of gravity dictates that person's destiny. But the spirit world operates on a superior level that transcends our laws of physics. This makes it a little difficult to describe things like demon possession or oppression because the spirit world is not confined to space and time. For instance, the Holy Sprit lives in every believer at the same time, so when we say things like, "Our bodies are the temple of the Holy Spirit, and He will never leave or forsake us," the ramifications of this are quite different than our finite definition of a person living in a house and never leaving.

I have observed things during deliverances that defy the laws of physics. I have literally seen with my own eyes people bending 180 degrees where there is no joint! I am not exaggerating—I have watched things happen during deliverance sessions that boggle the mind and have no earthly explanation. For those of you who have not experienced or observed these manifestations, these stories may seem hard to swallow. Nevertheless, they are true.

Another reason why the behavior of the spirit world is difficult to define is that demons are lawless. Much like criminals in our world who break the laws of the land, evil spirits often break God's spiritual laws. As we will see later in this chapter, much deliverance ministry involves simply policing the spirit realm by enforcing God's principles.

Necromancy

Necromancy means talking to the dead. I mentioned earlier that we are new creations in Christ. Our old man was buried in baptism, and our sin nature was crucified with Christ. Yet some believers insist on talking to the dead, their old man. They seem obsessed with the graveyard of their past as they hang out among the tombs of the dead. They have forgotten the angel's exhortation to Mary, "Why do you seek the living One among the dead?" (Luke 24:5). Like Lazarus, these believers have exited the tomb but remain bound with the grave clothes of their old flesh (see John 11:44). The deeds of the old man lead to the new man being demonically oppressed! The apostle Paul spoke of these grave diggers in Galatians 5:19–21:

> Now the *deeds of the flesh* are evident, which are: immorality, impurity, sensuality, idolatry, *sorcery*, enmities, strife, jealousy, outbursts of anger, disputes, dissensions, factions, envying, drunkenness, carousing, and things like these, of which I forewarn you, just as I have forewarned you, that those who practice such things will not inherit the kingdom of God [emphasis added].

Notice how human sin opens the door for sorcery and witchcraft to invade our lives. The best scriptural example of this is found in the relationship between King Saul and David. The armies of Israel were returning home from one of the greatest victories in their history. They had just defeated their archenemies, the Philistines. David had killed the mighty giant Goliath, which resulted in a Philistine rout. As the victorious Israeli army returned home from battle, the women lined the streets of Jerusalem to welcome their brave soldiers with singing and dancing. The mood was jubilant and celebratory, until King Saul heard the chorus line, "Saul has slain his thousands, and David his ten thousands" (1 Samuel 18:7).

Fear and jealousy flooded through King Saul. Enraged, he whined to himself, "They have ascribed to David ten thousands, but to me they have ascribed thousands. Now what more can he have but my kingdom?" (verse 8). The young man who once exuded humility was now an aging king, racked with fear and oppressed with demons. Here is Samuel's account of his dejected king:

> It came about on the next day that an evil spirit from God came mightily upon Saul, and he raved in the midst of the house, while David was playing the harp with his hand, as usual; and a spear was in Saul's hand. Saul hurled the spear for he thought, "I will pin David to the wall." But David escaped from his presence twice. Now Saul was afraid of David, for the LORD was with him but had departed from Saul.
>
> 1 Samuel 18:10–12

Paul reminds us in Galatians 5:21 that people who live a lifestyle of sin will not inherit the Kingdom of God! Much like the story that Jesus told in Matthew 18, where the torturers imprisoned the unforgiving servant, jealousy and fear can also release tormentors into our lives. Saul's life is a perfect example of how jealousy blinds us to reality and leads us to form irrational conclusions that finally incarcerate our souls.

Captives Liberated

To recap what we have learned so far, when we are working to free people who are demonized, we must first determine why they are bound—are they captives or prisoners? Prisoners are people who have invited demonic oppression into their lives through a lifestyle of sin. The demons know they have permission to wreak havoc in these prisoners' souls until the prisoners repent. Once a prisoner has repented, the evil spirits no longer have authorization to oppress that person because the roots of sin have been dealt with. In deliverance, a simple command to "get out" should cause the demons to leave and the person to be set free.

Now let's look at freeing captives. Captives are people who have been captured in battle and held as POWs. These people do not have lifestyle sin issues in their hearts. Instead, they are bound by lies they have believed. Jesus said, "You will know the truth, and the truth will make you free" (John 8:32). The word *truth* here means "reality." So many of us live in a "virtual reality"—it feels real and looks real, but it is not real. It is just an illusion. We give the devil permission to punish us because we think his lies are true. When we are tormented because of lies, we need a revelation of the truth of God so that we can break the steel bars of deception.

This testimony will help clarify my point. One day I was teaching upstairs in Bethel's School of Supernatural Ministry, and about halfway through my sermon someone came running up to me with an urgent message. We ran downstairs together, finally arriving at our counseling office. About eight people were fervently praying outside the room. I opened the office door to a wild scene. A very large woman was face-down on the floor, with one of our strongest maintenance workers on top of her, trying to restrain her. Two of our counselors were standing up against the wall, with the lady's arms wrapped around their legs. She was biting their shoes and growling at them.

The first question in my mind was, *Why do the demons have permission to torment this woman? Was she a prisoner who had sin and/or forgiveness issues in her life, or was she a captive who believed a lie?*

I got down on the floor and began to ask the Holy Spirit for insight into her bondage. Suddenly I heard Him say, *When she was a little girl, she was told that she blasphemed the Holy Spirit and was therefore banished to hell.* The Spirit continued, *It's a lie. I have forgiven her.*

I leaned over and whispered in her ear, "The devil told you when you were a little girl that you blasphemed the Holy Spirit, but it's a lie! You never did that. Renounce that lie."

The woman immediately calmed down and began to laugh. Within seconds she was completely delivered. Knowing the truth will make you free!

Breaking Contracts with Evil Spirits

It was early Sunday morning, and the worship team was taking us on a Holy Spirit journey. Sitting in the front row, I felt compelled to begin walking among the congregation and blessing them. The sanctuary was full of people standing and singing . . . completely lost in worship. I slowly moved in and out of the crowd, trying not to disturb anyone while I gently touched and blessed people. About halfway through the crowd, I noticed an elderly couple worshiping directly in front of me. They had been members of our church for over thirty years. I came up behind them and lightly laid my hands on their shoulders. They turned their heads toward me to see who was touching them. We smiled as our eyes met, and they continued to worship. But something strange happened when I put my hands on the wife, Martha. I heard the word *suicide* in my spirit. Martha was the last person in the world that I would have thought was struggling with suicide. She was happy and had a reputation as a wise and committed Christian.

I decided to take a risk. I leaned over and whispered in her ear, "Martha, by any chance are you dealing with suicidal thoughts?"

She opened her eyes and nodded, acknowledging that she was struggling with suicide. Tears rolled down her weathered cheeks as she leaned over and whispered in my ear, "I've been plagued with the thought that I should kill myself for nearly two months. I've never been suicidal in my entire life! I'm a happy and stable person, so I don't know why I'm having these horrible thoughts."

"Martha, did you go through something painful recently and entertain the thought that you could just die and all the grief would be gone?" I probed.

Her eyes widened, and the tone of her voice intensified. "Yes . . . yes, that's right . . . that's exactly what happened! I was really going through a hard time with one of my grand-kids a couple months ago. The situation was so desperate and it hurt so badly that I said to myself, *I could just die in peace and this would all be over.*"

"Did the terrible sense that you wanted to take your own life start right after that?" I asked.

"Yes!" she said, forgetting to whisper.

"Martha, when you chose to embrace death to bring peace, you made a covenant with the spirit of suicide to comfort you," I explained. "The devil's ministry is to steal, kill and destroy. Whenever we embrace one of these three elements that is his ministry, we invite demonic spirits to oppress us."

I put my arms around her to comfort her. Martha laid her head on my shoulder and said quietly, "How do I get free?"

"Repeat this prayer after me," I instructed. "Jesus, forgive me for making a covenant with the devil by inviting death to comfort me. Thank You that You gave me the Holy Spirit, who is my comforter and my friend."

She did that, and I went on, "Now, repeat this: You spirit of suicide, I break my agreement with you. I no longer want you in my life. I command you to leave me now in Jesus' name!"

Martha did that, too. A few seconds passed, and then she began to laugh. "It's gone!" she said loudly enough for her husband to hear. "It's really gone!"

About a month later, I saw her in church again. She came right up to me and gave me a hug. "Thank you so much for helping me get free from that suicide thing," she said excitedly. I did not really have to ask her if she was still free . . . her face told the whole story.

Besides a lifestyle of sin and believing lies, negative covenants are one of the most common ways that Christians invite demonic oppression into their lives. Any time we turn to the devil's devices to solve the issues of our soul, we step out from under the umbrella of God's protection and become vulnerable to the elements. Freedom comes, as I shared in the story above, by breaking these covenants through verbally renouncing each one of them. When these contracts are destroyed, our enemy loses the legal right to oppress us.

Authority

When God created the world, He put humans in charge, commanding them to rule "over all the earth" (Genesis 1:26). As I said before, when Adam and Eve sinned, it was not just a matter of disobeying God—they changed masters by obeying the serpent. The earth was no longer "one planet under God, ruled by man." Instead, Adam and Eve gave their ruling rights to the devil. When Jesus was led into the wilderness to war against Satan, the devil said to Him, "I will give You all this domain and its glory; *for it has been handed over to me*, and I give it to whomever I wish" (Luke 4:6, emphasis added). The devil was right; he had deceived Adam and Eve into giving him their authority to rule the world.

Because God gave humankind the dominion of the earth, it would take a human to get it back. When Jesus obeyed God by dying on the cross as a man, He wrestled the keys of dominion away from the devil. That is why when He rose from the dead, Jesus said, "*All authority* has been given to Me in heaven and on earth. Go therefore and make disciples of all the nations" (Matthew 28:18–19, emphasis added). Jesus restored our original commission to rule the earth.

It is important to note that Jesus said He had *"All authority."* If Jesus has all authority, that would mean that Satan has none! We are in Christ, therefore we carry His authority into every circumstance, every geographic location and every situation. The only way that Satan has authority is when

155

we give it to him. That is why he works so hard to get us to empower him through lies, sin or covenant agreements.

When believers refuse to listen to the devil, however, he becomes a powerless pawn of God's divine purposes. I will leave you with this thought from Ephesians 4:27: "Do not give the devil an opportunity."

10

Generational Curses

Joshua, commissioned by God to take the Promised Land, crossed the River Jordan and began his conquest around 1400 B.C. He supernaturally ransacked Jericho, a fortified city protected by dual walls. Next, after recovering from a miscue that was the result of sin, the Israelites destroyed Ai. Rumors began to circulate throughout the entire land of Canaan as the Israelis conquered city after city.

When word got back to the Gibeonites that Joshua was on the move toward their city, they were terrified. They devised a plan to try to convince the Israelites to make a covenant with them. The Gibeonites dressed up in old, worn-out clothes, put on raunchy sandals, grabbed some stale food and went out to meet Joshua. They told him they were from a faraway land and had heard of the fame of the Lord and the greatness of His people, so they had come out to honor the Israelites. Of course, they were lying their faces off, but Joshua did not know it because he forgot to ask God about them. With a little razzle-dazzle, they convinced Joshua and the elders of Israel to make a covenant with them and let them live. Three days later, Joshua found out he had been deceived. The Israelites wanted to destroy Gibeon, but the elders reminded the people that their word was their bond (see Joshua 9:3–18).

Fast-forward four hundred years to the reign of King David. There was a severe famine in the land, and David was distraught but did not know what to do. Finally, after three years, he decided to ask God why there was a famine. (You would think with all that tabernacle time, that the guy would be a little quicker to talk to the Lord about his problems. I guess even in those days, men refused to ask for directions.) The Lord answered David and said:

> "It is for Saul and his bloody house, because he put the Gibeonites to death."
> So the king called the Gibeonites and spoke to them (now the Gibeonites were not of the sons of Israel but of the remnant of the Amorites, and the sons of Israel made a covenant with them, *but Saul had sought to kill them in his zeal for the sons of Israel and Judah*).
>
> 2 Samuel 21:1–2, emphasis added

Let's make sure we understand what happened. Joshua mistakenly made a covenant with Gibeon and let them live in the Promised Land, against God's direct orders. About 370 years later, King Saul murdered the Gibeonites because of his zeal for the people of God. Later, Saul dies in battle and David becomes king. He reigned for many years before encountering this serious famine. But when the famine occurred, he asked God for direction, which led him to uncover a family curse that occurred in the previous generation. In other words, it had not rained in three years, the crops were failing, the sheep and cattle were dying and Israel was forced into a depression all because a long-dead king had sinned against the Gibeonites. It was Joshua who screwed up and disobeyed God. It was Saul who broke a multigenerational Israeli covenant with the Gibeonites to commit genocide against them. But it was David who reaped the effects of their sins. This is what is called a "generational curse," and many people are unknowingly affected by them today.

My Story

Let me take you back to my nightmare in the bathtub and share with you "the rest of the story" that I have been keeping from you until now. Do you remember in chapter 1 I told you about a panic attack that I had that lasted over three years? It had started with the intense thought, *I am going to die!*

In the third year of my nervous breakdown, I was in a hotel room in Los Angeles. I had just bought that Union 76 station, and the company required me to attend a week of training. I had never flown before, and to make matters worse, I had serious claustrophobia. When I finally arrived at the hotel room in downtown L.A., I was a basket case. Now I had to spend a week in my hotel room by myself. I was terrified of being alone in a big city. The torment that week intensified as I fought off the spirit of death. Then one night toward the end of the week, in the midst of this warfare, I asked God, "How did this spirit of death get access to my life?"

Immediately I heard the Lord say, *A man was in love with your mother when she was young, and he convinced her to let him read tarot cards for her. Out of jealousy, he cursed*

159

your family, killing your father and sabotaging your mother's future.

I was floored! It was past midnight, yet I was compelled to call my mother. She answered the phone half asleep, but she listened intently as I recounted what the Lord had shown me. Then I said, "Mom, do you know anything at all about the situation?"

There was a long pause. I could hear my mother weeping on the other end of the phone. "Mom . . . Mother, do you know anything about this?" I pressed.

"Yes," she said, her voice quivering. "When I was a teenager and was dating your father, a much older man fell in love with me. He was a close friend of your grandfather's and was very jealous of your father. One day he came over to our house and asked if he could read my future. I was young and ignorant, and I had no idea what he was really doing. I did not want to disappoint him, so I agreed. He pulled out a deck of tarot cards and began to tell me about my future.

"'You will be married three times,' he proclaimed. 'Your first marriage will end in disaster, and your other two marriages will be filled with trouble.'"

By now, my mother was weeping uncontrollably on the phone.

"Mom, do you realize that this man did not just tell your future . . . he caused it!" I told her. "He cursed you, releasing evil spirits to carry out his declarations!"

"Yes, I realize that now," she confessed. She went on to tell me more of the story. "Six months before your father drowned in Anderson Dam, he woke up every night screaming, *'I'm going to die! I'm going to die! I know I'm going to die!'* I would try so hard to comfort him, but nothing seemed to help," she said, as if reliving a nightmare. "Although he was an excellent swimmer, a few months later he drowned."

"Mom, you need to ask God to forgive you for allowing that man to read tarot cards for you. I realize that you allowed it in your innocence and ignorance, but it still opened a door of destruction to our family lineage. The curse of the fear of death has passed down to me and my children, and it is trying to kill me, as it did my father."

That night my mother repented for her sin and renounced any covenant she had made with that man through embracing his words. Little did I know that this would lay a foundation for my deliverance that would take place just a few months later.

The spirit of death would prove a formidable enemy throughout my family's lives. My son Jason and my daughter Jaime have both experienced severe assaults from this spirit. Yet when my mother repented, the family curse was broken. The enemy no longer had an invitation or the right to harass and oppress us. Solomon put it like this: "The undeserved curse doesn't come to rest" (Proverbs 26:2, WEB). When Jesus died on the cross, He became *the* curse for us so that He could release us from *all* curses (see Galatians 3:13). The devil and his demons no longer have the right to torment believers. But they are lawless criminals of the spirit realm. They will break God's laws whenever and wherever they see a lack of authority. Like the city of New Orleans after Hurricane Katrina, where thousands of looters ravaged people's homes in the absence of officers policing the streets, demonic spirits will illegally ravage the lives of people in the vacuum of true spiritual authority. Ignorant Christians create powerless cultures, resulting in the world experiencing an unrestrained devil!

I think it is important to explain the difference between power and authority. A police officer exemplifies someone with both power and authority. His gun gives him power, but it is his badge that gives him authority.

The Greek word for power is *dunamis*, which means "miraculous strength, might or power." The Greek word for authority is *exousia*, which means "the right to act, jurisdiction, dominion or to be in charge." Jesus said, "Behold, I have given you authority [Greek word *exousia*] to tread on serpents and scorpions, and over all the power [Greek word *dunamis*] of the enemy, and nothing will injure you" (Luke 10:19). Then in Acts 1:8, Jesus said, "You will receive power [Greek word *dunamis*] when the Holy Spirit has come upon you."

Make no mistake about it, the devil has power, strength, might and the ability to do miracles (called false signs and wonders), but he has no authority. Christians have authority over the power of the demonic world, and we have power that is greater than the power of the devil! Whenever evil spirits are exercising power over a believer, they are trespassing on God's property (unless, of course, believers invite them onto their homesteads, as I explained in the previous chapter).

Breaking Generational Curses

It is easy to break generational curses when the people who created them are still alive and are willing to repent for their sins. But what do you do if your family, city or nation is under a generational curse and the people who caused the curse are dead or unrepentant? The answer is "identificational repentance." Identificational repentance breaks generational curses. A great example of identificational repentance occurs in the life of the Israelites during the days of Nehemiah. The Israelites had rebuilt the Temple, but they had been unable to build the walls and gates around their city, as I described in chapter 3. When Nehemiah heard of the destructive condition of his home country, he realized that this was a curse brought on by his forefathers' sin, so he prayed this prayer:

> *We have sinned against You; I and my father's house have sinned. We have acted very corruptly against You and have not kept the commandments, nor the statutes, nor the ordinances which You commanded Your servant Moses.* Remember the word which You commanded Your servant Moses, saying, "If you are unfaithful I will scatter you among the peoples; but if you return to Me and keep My commandments and do them, though those of you who have been scattered were in the most remote part of the heavens, I will gather them from there and will bring them to the place where I have chosen to cause My name to dwell."
>
> Nehemiah 1:6–9, emphasis added

Believe it or not, the key word in Nehemiah's prayer is *we!* It was not Nehemiah who sinned, it was his forefathers. But he took responsibility for their sin so that the people could reap the benefit of his repentance. When Nehemiah embraced his forefathers' sin as his own, he was able to repent as if he were a partaker of their actions and attitudes.

The same principle was established in the pattern of redemption. One lamb was offered each year for an entire family. The apostle Paul pulled this principle into the new covenant when he said, "The unbelieving husband is sanctified through his [believing] wife, and the unbelieving wife is sanctified through her believing husband; for otherwise your children are unclean, but now they are holy" (1 Corinthians 7:14). In other words, one believer's righteous stand has the power to break the curses off anyone in their metron, or sphere of authority (see chapter 3). Of course, I do not mean that when we receive Christ our whole family is saved, but instead of curses, they do experience the blessings of a superior Kingdom as long as they remain under our covering.

I personally believe that when we receive Christ, every curse, no matter its origin, should automatically be broken over our lives. We have become a new creation and old things have passed away. We have been given a new heart and a new mind. We are of the royal bloodline of Jesus Christ. Generational sins, hereditary diseases and systemic poverty are not a part of our royal status. Yet in reality, trespassing demonic spirits oftentimes stymie the full benefits of our inheritance. It is up to us to understand our rights and police the heavens. Remember that the devil is an equal opportunity destroyer!

The Child Is a Warrior

Islamic terrorists are training children in battle techniques and teaching them to fight for their cause. Homosexuals and pornographers have created elaborate strategies to capture the hearts of our children. But for some reason, it has not occurred to most Christians that children do not receive a junior Holy Spirit. The full arsenal of the weapons of our warfare are available to kids of all ages. King Solomon wrote, "Behold, children are a gift of the LORD, the fruit of the womb is a reward. *Like arrows in the hand of a warrior*, so are the children of one's youth" (Psalm 127:3–4, emphasis added).

Children were born to be arrows in the hands of warriors. They pierce deep into the darkness as they impact the hearts of our enemies.

Christian schools have often become comfortable sanctuaries where children are sheltered from the devices of the devil, instead of becoming Holy Spirit terrorist training centers that sharpen these arrows for the destruction of evil forces. It is time that we give our children more than a Happy Meal. We need to teach them how to deal with the destructive forces of evil from the time they are little. Kingdom combat training should be part of every homeschooler's life, every Christian school's curriculum and every parent's instruction.

It should be obvious to all of us that evil spirits are not selective with their destructive devices. For some reason, Christians seem surprised when little children come under extreme assaults. Satan hates children today maybe more than he has in any other generation. When Moses was a baby, the devil wiped out an entire generation of kids in a ruthless attempt to destroy him. When Jesus was a baby, the devil did it again. And now, the greatest holocaust in human history is taking place in the womb of women as thousands of helpless children are aborted every single day.

Mesha

Ten years ago, I received a deep revelation of the enemy's destructive purposes toward children. My oldest granddaughter, Mesha, has seen angels since the time that she could talk. She used to call them "birds." She had been describing these "birds" in her limited vocabulary for months. Because she was only two years old, we thought she was just pretending.

Then one morning, Mesha was taking a bath with her mother. The presence of God filled the bathroom like a cloud. Mesha stood up in the tub and shouted, *"The birds are here . . . the birds are here!"* Oftentimes we would catch her in the bedroom interacting with the angels, as a person would play with friends. As she has gotten older, her angelic experiences have grown more exciting and intense.

When Mesha was about four, she began to wake up in the middle of the night screaming, *"The angels are scaring me!"* This went on several times a night for weeks on end. My daughter and son-in-law, who are pastors, would run to her room and try unsuccessfully to console her. It was not long before they were calling me at two and three o'clock in the morning. One night, when we had already been up a couple of times praying with her, I told them to ask her what color the angels were.

"Dad, she says they're black!"

"Oh," I mused, "I bet they're demons. Tell Mesha to command the demons to go outside."

A few seconds later, I heard a tiny voice shout, *"Go outside! Go outside now!"*

The demons left, only to return the next night. At three o'clock, Jaime and Marty woke to Mesha shouting, *"Go outside, you bad angels! Leave now!"*

They rushed to her room, only to see little Mesha standing in the dark on her bed, pointing outside in a stern voice and commanding the demons to go outside. When they turned the light on, Mesha excitedly said, "I made the black angels go outside."

Mesha is twelve years old as of this writing, and she has never been afraid of demons again. She has rarely ever been assaulted after that second night of commanding the demons to leave.

It is hard to imagine, but I am convinced that demons are more afraid of children than they are of adults. There is something about childlike faith and innocence that God protects in an extraordinary way!

11

On-the-Job Training

I want to give you a little *on-the-job training* in this chapter, primarily based on my experience in helping people get free from demonic strongholds. In the two previous chapters, we talked about different ways in which Christians invite or allow demonic oppression. Now I want to talk about a few practical things to remember when casting evil spirits out of people. First of all, never expel demons from someone who does not know the Lord. If you are ministering to people who do not know Jesus, lead them to Christ first before you try to set them free.

Am I saying Christians are the only people whom we should set free? Well, yes and no. Let me explain what I mean by quoting Jesus:

> When the unclean spirit goes out of a man, it passes through waterless places seeking rest, and does not find it. Then it says, "I will return to my house from which I came"; and when it

comes, it finds it unoccupied, swept, and put in order. Then it goes and takes along with it seven other spirits more wicked than itself, and they go in and live there; and the last state of that man becomes worse than the first.

Matthew 12:43–45

The Lord makes it clear in this passage that when an evil spirit is forced out of a person's life, it always returns with reinforcements more wicked than itself, with whom it tries to bully its way back into the person's body. If it finds its old house unoccupied, those eight evil spirits move in, and the person becomes worse off than when only one evil spirit was present. Casting evil spirits out of people who do not have, or do not want to have, the Holy Spirit in their lives is therefore irresponsible and dangerous. Many people do not believe in casting demons out of Christians, but I am telling you, Christians are the only people you *should* set free.

Let's say you run into someone who does not know the Lord and is really tormented. What should you do? Simple— lead them to Christ, get them baptized in the Holy Spirit and then give them a spiritual cleansing. Most often you will find that when a person receives Jesus, the torment automatically stops. But if it remains, walk the person through the steps you learned in chapter 9, and then command the demons to leave them.

After you command the evil spirits to leave, the person should feel free and peaceful. If that is not the case, ask the Holy Spirit if there is any other reason why the person is still troubled. The Holy Spirit is really good at revealing the root issues at the foundation of demonic strongholds. Have the person deal with the issues God uncovers. After that, command the spirits to leave again. Like a weed, when the root is cut, the plant will die. Continue this process until the person feels free and peaceful.

At this point, it is important to reassure people that you also discern that they are free. I like to look into their eyes and let them know that I see a clean heart and a free soul. You want them to leave with faith in their deliverance, so your reassurance is vital to their well-being.

It is also important that we teach those who get set free that evil spirits will often come back to visit, along with their demonic co-destroyers, and knock on the door of a freed person's heart. This is nothing to worry about; it is just a normal part of spiritual cleansing. Instruct people to keep their minds on the Lord and not go to the land of asking, *What did I do wrong to invite these spirits back into my life?* Witch-hunting in our souls plays right into the schemes of the devil. He is not called the accuser of the brethren for nothing. He is the master repossessor, convincing people that their newfound freedom is undeserved. In my experience, these demonic revisitations usually occur three or four times over in the first few months of a person's freedom, and then they usually leave the person alone for good. Remember that God's ability to protect us is much greater than any of our enemies' powers to destroy us. Anyone who gets delivered should memorize Paul's words in Romans 8:37–39:

> In all these things we overwhelmingly conquer through Him who loved us. For I am convinced that neither death, nor life, nor angels, nor principalities, nor things present, nor things to come, nor powers, nor height, nor depth, nor any other created thing, will be able to separate us from the love of God, which is in Christ Jesus our Lord.

Discerning Evil Spirits

Many people ask me, "How do you know what kind of demons are oppressing people?" You can determine the nature of the evil spirits in a couple of different ways. One way is through the manifestation of the torment or bondage. If a person is plagued with thoughts of suicide, as in the example I gave about Martha, the bondage is probably rooted in a spirit of suicide.

The other way to identify what kind of spirit is tormenting a person is through the gift of discernment (see 1 Corinthians 12:10). This gift, also called the distinguishing of spirits in some translations of the Bible, is a free gift of the Holy Spirit. You cannot earn it; you can only ask for it. It is available to every Christian.

The gift of discernment operates differently through various people. The most common way this gift manifests in us is that we feel, hear, smell or taste whatever spirit is troubling the person whose metron we are in.

Before we get deeper into the subject of discernment, we need to refresh our memories about metrons and the spheres of authority I talked about briefly in chapter 3. This concept comes from the meaning of two Greek words. The first is *metron*, meaning "measure" or "standard." The second is *kanon*, meaning "to rule a sphere." Both words are used in Paul's exhortation to the Corinthians. Read it slowly:

> We will not boast beyond our *measure* [Greek root word *metron*], but within the *measure* [*metron*] of the *sphere* [Greek word *kanon*] which God apportioned to us as a *measure* [*metron*], to reach even as far as you . . . not boasting beyond our *measure* [*metron*], that is, in other men's labors, but with

the hope that as your faith grows, we will be, within our *sphere* [*kanon*], enlarged even more by you.

2 Corinthians 10:13, 15, emphasis added

Simply stated, Paul is saying that the people of Corinth are within the boundaries of his God-given spiritual authority. Unfortunately, the occultists and New Age people are the only ones I know who have a vocabulary for this concept. They call it an *aura*. They believe people have an aura around them that influences the atmosphere surrounding them. In truth, this is a biblical concept. Every person has a metron (measured space) that he or she rules over or influences. The size of people's metrons is determined by their God-given spiritual influence. A metron can be restricted to the size of an individual, or it can be as large as his or her sphere of authority.

For example, have you ever walked into a store and immediately felt exhausted? You quickly purchased the things you needed and left. As soon as you got into your vehicle and drove away, you were fine . . . the tired feeling had lifted. Most likely, the manager or owner of that store had a spirit of fatigue or fainting. (Isaiah 61:3 says that the Lord will give us "the mantle of praise instead of a spirit of fainting.") Because *all* authority is from God and it is He who determines the size of a person's metron (see Romans 13:1; 2 Corinthians 10:13–15), an owner's or manager's metron would be the size of the store. When you walked into the store, you actually were entering the spiritual space of the person in authority there, and you were discerning the ruling spirits the person had invited into that "space."

On a personal level, if you have the gift of discernment and you sit next to someone troubled by an evil spirit of pornography, you most likely will experience pornographic thoughts or pictures while you are in that person's "space." Or if you touch someone dealing with a demon of depression, you suddenly will feel depressed. I should make it clear that the spirit realm affects all Christians, whether they are aware of it or not. The gift of discernment simply gives you the ability to distinguish what spirit or spirits are at work in a person or an environment.

Counseling Tools

When I first joined the staff at Bethel Church, one of my main responsibilities was counseling. When people would come into my office for counsel, I would lay hands on them and pray before I let them tell me why they came to see me. I would pray for wisdom and insight, but honestly, what I was really doing was touching them so that I could discern if an evil spirit was involved in their situation. If I laid hands on a person and I was not troubled by something, then I knew whatever the counselee was dealing with was purely human and not demonic. On the other hand, if I felt rage, murder, hatred, fear, paranoia or any other negative manifestation, I knew that evil spirits had attached themselves to the situation and therefore counseling alone would not solve the person's issue. We would have to make sure that we expelled the evil spirits after we dealt with the root causes of their invitation.

While we are on the subject, let me make it clear that people can get themselves into some terrible situations without the devil's help. Pornography, hatred and depression, for example, are not necessarily manifestations of evil spirits. Oftentimes these are the fruit of people's own choices. But if demons have somehow been attracted to a person, circumstance or place, talking alone will not solve the problem!

A while ago I was teaching our church about the ministry of deliverance and the gift of discernment, and I shared how I touch people to discern if they are troubled by evil spirits. At the end of my message, when I stood at the back door to greet people as they left, I noticed that most of them changed directions and went out the opposite exit. For several minutes I was bewildered by their behavior, until one brave soul came to the door, extended his hand, and said, "Pastor, if you sense an evil spirit in me, just make it leave!"

I realized then that people were exiting from the opposite door because they thought I might sense that they were demonized. That made me laugh so hard! Now I am more discreet when I share my examples from the podium.

Bipolar?

The ability to distinguish evil spirits is an awesome tool that can help people get free. But if you do not understand how to use this equipment, it can make you feel crazy. I think many Christians with a strong gift of discernment are diagnosed with a bipolar disorder because they do not know they are gifted. They think they are experiencing mood swings, but they do not understand that they are simply sensing the spiritual atmosphere in a particular metron.

While we are talking about discernment, I also want to warn you about suspicion. Suspicion is discernment's wicked stepsister. It can masquerade as discernment and ultimately lead us into bondage. Suspicion is the gift of discernment being used by the spirit of fear. For example, before King Saul was tormented by demons, the Bible says that "Saul looked at David with suspicion from that day on" (1 Samuel 18:9). Suspicion leads to bitterness, unforgiveness and torment; it will result in a person being cast into a spiritual prison where all the guards work for the dark side. The spirits who guard the bars of this prison have names like sickness, depression, hatred and murder.

Many times over the past several years, I have literally watched suspicion in action as someone "discerned" that a person had an evil spirit of one kind or another and proceeded to destroy that person's reputation. When I first came to Bethel Church, one of our "prophetic people" "discerned" that a leading government official in our city was secretly a witch. The prophetic person freely circulated this information to several prominent people in our church for "prayer." A year later, I got to know that city official and discovered that he was actually a strong believer who loved God. But our church member's "insight" had already poisoned me, so I stood aloof from him. It took me a long time to realize that what was being sold as the "gift of discernment" was actually suspicion rooted in a different political perspective.

When you have a strong negative opinion about someone, do not trust your "gift of discernment." Solomon said that a good name is more desirable than great wealth (see Proverbs 22:1). The goal of any gift of the Spirit is to build trust and help people grow in God. No gift of the Spirit should be used to destroy people's reputations, kill their passion for God or steal their identity. Even if your discernment proves accurate and a demonic spirit is troubling a person, that person's reputation should be protected and his or her personhood should always be honored as someone created in the likeness of God.

No Fear

When helping someone get free from demonic oppression, it is important that you are confident in God's power to deliver. If you become afraid in a deliverance session, the evil spirits will sense your anxiety. They will know that you do not have faith for their victim's freedom, and they will refuse to leave. I have watched people try to overcome their fear of an evil spirit by yelling at the demons to come out. Raising your voice will not increase your authority. Demons do not respond to anger, manipulation or control. They only respond to authority. In Acts, Paul's hankie expelled demons (see Acts 19:11–12). No yelling, no name-calling, no drama, just a hankie! Contrary to popular opinion, it is the unclean spirit that sometimes cries out with a loud voice as it is leaving a person (see Mark 1:26).

I remember one time that I was praying for a huge guy in a prayer line at church. As soon as I put my hand on his shoulder, a strange voice shouted at me, *"I've been here for generations and I'm not coming out!"*

"I don't care how long you've been there, you're coming out," I said quietly but confidently.

"No I'm not!" the voice yelled louder.

"Oh yes you are," I responded.

"I'm going to kill you!" the voice shouted as the man swung at me with his right hand. He encountered an impregnable force about a quarter inch from my face. I stood there confidently looking into his eyes.

He screamed, growled and yelled at the top of his lungs, *"You're dead!"* Then he pulled his left hand back and threw me a haymaker! I could feel the wind from his fist as it neared my face. *Boooooom!* His fist slammed into something invisible but solid! This enraged the evil spirit in him.

177

"It's my turn," I announced. I put my hand on his head and said, "I call for the fire of God to burn up this man's enemies! Fire, more fire, baptize this man in fire!" I said boldly.

The big guy began to vibrate like a jackhammer. For four or five minutes, he literally vibrated up and down, screaming and yelling, while I calmly kept my hand on his head, praying for the fire of God to fill his soul.

Finally a loud voice screamed out of him, *"Satan, help me! Satan, please help me!"*

"He's not helping you. Now get out!" I said sternly.

A few seconds later, the spirit threw him on the floor and left. The man was free, and now we had to make sure that the doors were closed so that no more evil spirits could come back.

Deliverance Manifestations

People experience many different kinds of manifestations when they are getting free. You cannot measure the level of someone's freedom by the amount of drama a demon displays in exiting. In fact, the most freedom is usually experienced with the least amount of deliverance drama. A person may hardly feel the unclean spirit leave, but may feel a huge weight lift off or have a new sense of intense peace.

The person's dignity should be our priority during any session. I always try to make people feel safe and loved as we work to get them free. Demons love attention, so they like to make as big a scene as possible when leaving. When those ministering deliverance ask evil spirits their names or make a person throw up or do anything else that creates anxiety and drama, it just plays into the demons' evil devices. Even asking the demon its name is rarely necessary. Unless you are Jesus, they will probably lie to you anyway.

In deliverance situations, stay calm, speak in a normal voice and remain confident. The demons have to leave when we unearth the root cause of their attraction. Remember, you have been anointed to release captives and free prisoners!

Principalities and Powers

Although the scope of this book primarily involves personal warfare, I feel prompted to give you some of my insights on the broader scale of principalities and powers. I feel I have been able to write with great authority up until this point, since the things I have taught so far have come out of my own personal experience of living out the Word of God in my life. I am confident what I have written up to this point is true because I lived it. The rest of this chapter is subjective, as my experience is limited in this area. Nevertheless, I offer the following thoughts for your consideration.

Go back with me to the subject of metrons and spheres of authority that we covered in the last chapter, and let me offer you some insight into warring against principalities and powers. Did you notice that when we studied the armor of God earlier, we learned that "our struggle is not against flesh and blood, but against the rulers, against the powers, against the world forces of this darkness, against the spiritual forces of wickedness in the heavenly places" (Ephesians 6:12)? The wrestling match we face in the "standing" seasons of our lives is not simply against demons. Read the verse again—our battle is against *rulers*, *powers*, *world forces of darkness* and *spiritual forces of wickedness*.

Remember that Jesus said when a demon is cast out, seven spirits *more evil than the first* will attempt to return. Levels of authority exist in the demonic, much as they do in the natural world. High-ranking demons are often referred to as *principalities and powers*. Paul put it like this:

> You were dead in your trespasses and sins, in which you formerly walked according to the course of this world, according to the prince of the power of the air, of the spirit that is now working in the sons of disobedience.
>
> Ephesians 2:1–2

In Romans 8:38–39, Paul reassures us that principalities and powers cannot separate us from the love of God. These principalities and powers are dominant evil spirits that have large metrons and spheres. Paul teaches us in Ephesians that four types of ruling principalities war against us. These are not your typical demons—these are high-level evil spirits who are grasping at authority over geographic and demographic territories. In other words, they want to rule cities, nations or industries like pornography. But they only have authority if believers give it to them. For example, Jesus told Christians to disciple nations. The way that principalities gain authority over a nation is for believers to vacate their God-given metrons and spheres.

Eradicating Spiritual Air Pollution

Jesus came across this situation in the country of the Gerasenes when He got out of a boat and encountered a demon-possessed man. Jesus said, "Come out of the man, you unclean spirit!" When He asked him, "What is your name?" the man replied, "My name is Legion; for we are many." And then the man began to implore Jesus earnestly *"not to send them out of the country"* (Mark 5:8–10, emphasis added).

It is probable that territorial principalities were using that man, known as Legion, as a home base for their assaults against the country. The fact that that region was raising pigs gives us some insight into the corporate sin that probably opened the door for this historic assault. Swine were considered unclean under Old Testament law, and therefore were not to be raised. I am not proposing that just raising pigs opened the door for territorial spirits to rule the Gerasenes, but I am suggesting that the inhabitants' complete disrespect for the Word of God gave the principalities access to their country. Legion's personal deliverance led to an entire country receiving Christ later on.

Most of the armor of God described in Ephesians 6 is worn to protect us from these high-ranking spirits. We are instructed to "stand firm" during these assaults. So how do principalities actually get dethroned? Jesus' words in Luke 10:17–20 give us some insight into that question:

> The seventy returned with joy, saying, "Lord, even the demons are subject to us in Your name." And He said to them, "*I was watching Satan fall from heaven like lightning.* Behold, I have given you authority to tread on serpents and scorpions, and over all the power of the enemy, and nothing will injure you. Nevertheless do not rejoice in this, that the spirits are subject to you, but rejoice that your names are recorded in heaven [emphasis added]."

The seventy were casting demons out of people, but Jesus saw Satan falling from heaven like lightning. Contrary to popular opinion, lightning starts from the ground up. When demons are cast out of people in the natural realm (the ground level), territory is taken in the spiritual realm (the heavens) because all of us occupy two dimensions simultaneously. Principalities that rule the air are based in people. As these people get delivered, their spheres and realms gain freedom and the "spiritual air pollution" is eradicated. But my experience tells me that encountering a high-level evil prince in a person that is ruling a territory is quite different from dealing with a "regular demon." Getting people free who have become enslaved in this manner can be a wrestling match or a struggle, as Ephesians 6:12 puts it. Getting these kinds of people delivered will require you to be extremely vigilant, extra patient and very persistent.

The Samaritan Revival

Now let's take a look at Dr. Luke's account of the Samaritan revival and see if we can discover some similarities to what we have been talking about. Philip the evangelist went down to Samaria preaching the Kingdom, working miracles and casting out demons. Suddenly, he encountered a sorcerer named Simon. Here's his account:

> There was a man named Simon, who formerly was practicing magic in the city and astonishing the people of Samaria, claiming to be someone great; and they all, from smallest to greatest, were giving attention to him, saying, "This man is what is called the Great Power of God." And they were giving him attention because he had for a long time astonished them with his magic arts. But when they believed Philip preaching the good news about the kingdom of God and the name of

Jesus Christ, they were being baptized, men and women alike. Even Simon himself believed; and after being baptized, he continued on with Philip, and as he observed signs and great miracles taking place, he was constantly amazed.

Now when the apostles in Jerusalem heard that Samaria had received the word of God, they sent them Peter and John, who came down and prayed for them that they might receive the Holy Spirit.

Acts 8:9–15

Is it possible that the principality that ruled Samaria lived in Simon the sorcerer? When Simon accepted Christ, and when the apostles at Jerusalem heard that Samaria had embraced the Kingdom, they sent them Peter and John. The power of God displaced the power of the devil through the evangelistic ministry of Philip, and the government of God replaced the ruling principalities through the apostolic authority of Peter and John.

It is important to understand that when principalities fall like lightning over a city and no longer rule the minds of people, it is imperative that Kingdom authority replace these fallen princes. Otherwise, the condition of the city becomes worse than before, as demonic reinforcements try vigilantly to force their way back into the seat of authority.

Iraq provides a modern-day example of a power struggle over ruling territory. As I pointed out in *Heavy Rain*, my book that I mentioned earlier, the war in Iraq has taught us some profound lessons about this principle. We learned, and are still learning the hard way, that displacing an evil dictator is not nearly as difficult as replacing him. We overthrew Saddam Hussein in 37 days and declared victory from the deck of the aircraft carrier USS *Abraham Lincoln*. But we have spent several more years and the lives of many more soldiers trying to establish democracy in a country that has known only tyranny for hundreds of years. Terrorists have fought viciously to repossess authority in the country.

This is a clear picture in the natural realm of the way that spiritual principalities must be dealt with in the spiritual realm. Jesus never rebuked the ruling spirit over a city or country. He simply traveled from city to city, setting people free as He went. Freedom was rising from the ground up. And unbeknownst to most of the world, Satan was falling like lightning!

12

For the Love of God

After all of the oppression in my life and the years of helping other people get free, I am convinced that the root cause of *all* demonic activity is the absence of the love of God. John, called the apostle whom Jesus loved, said, "There is no fear in love; but perfect love casts out fear, because fear involves punishment, and the one who fears is not perfected in love" (1 John 4:18). If people really knew how much the Father loved them, and if they received His love in the depths of their souls, they would never allow themselves to be oppressed or tormented in any way.

The great apostle Paul put it this way: "For I am convinced that neither death, nor life, nor angels, nor *principalities*, nor things present, nor things to come, nor *powers*, nor height, nor depth, nor any other created thing, will be able to separate us from the love of God, which is in Christ Jesus our Lord" (Romans 8:38–39, emphasis added). The reality is that many believers can repeat these Bible verses, but they have never really experienced the love of the Father.

My Story

My father was the star football player and my mother was the head high-school cheerleader when they fell in love with each other. It was a fairy-tale love affair until my mother became pregnant with me out of wedlock. It was the fifties, a time when society attached a lot more shame to immorality than it does today. When my maternal grandfather found out that his daughter was pregnant, he disowned both my mom and my dad, even though they had run away and gotten married before I was born. A year later, my dad surprised my grandfather by coming to his back door . Before my grandfather had a chance to send him away, my dad dropped to his knees and begged for forgiveness. Thankfully, my grandfather forgave him that morning. Grandfather would prove indispensable to us in the disaster that soon followed.

Two years later, my father was fishing when a huge storm suddenly capsized the boat he was in. My father rescued my uncle and took him to shore, then went back to retrieve the boat. He never returned. As I mentioned in chapter 10, my father drowned, and on that stormy night in 1958 my life changed forever. When my father died, my grandfather made a covenant at the funeral that he would take care of us.

My mother remarried twice. Our first stepfather came into our lives when I was five and my sister was three. My new stepfather made it clear to us that we were the trash that came with the treasure. And as if that were not bad enough, he also was a violent alcoholic. Brutality and cruelty became a way of life for us. I spent all of my early years growing up trying to be invisible. Evidently, my stepfather had a similar goal for my biological father. He tried hard to rid us of all our memories of my dad. He destroyed all my dad's belongings and prohibited us from seeing any of his relatives. My mother finally divorced this man when I was thirteen. She remarried again when I was fifteen, but that situation was no better. The abuse continued.

My Grandfather

Although both stepfathers could hardly stand the sight of me, my grandfather loved me. My grandmother and grandfather owned four rickety old houses all situated on one large lot. When my father died, we moved into one of those houses, next door to my grandfather. In those days, my grandfather worked as a custodian at a high school. I spent a lot of time at home by myself while my mother worked to try to make ends meet. Every day I waited eagerly for my grandfather to get home from work in his black '53 Ford. I could hear the old Ford coming up the long driveway as I ran out to greet him. I would jump up and down . . . hang on his legs . . . pull on his arms . . . whatever it took to get his undivided attention. (You can imagine how hungry I was for male affection.)

My grandfather never seemed bothered or acted as if I were intruding on his time. He would rub his hand over my crew cut and say, "How was your day, knucklehead?" (Knucklehead was my grandfather's nickname for anyone he liked.) I would spend the rest of the day shadowing my grandfather as he worked around his houses. He had worked on a farm most of his life, which made his hands thick and yellow with calluses. When you shook his hand, it felt as if you were holding a leather glove. Grandpa stood about five-foot-six and was nearly as wide. I am not saying he was fat; he was just kind of stout. He did not really walk . . . he sort of waddled. He always wore a pair of old coveralls that he refused to button (although my grandma nagged him constantly about it). It is one of the first things that you would notice about my grandfather, because he did not wear underwear!

When I was young, my grandfather got a gum disease and had to have all his teeth pulled. For some reason, they left his four eyeteeth in his mouth and made dentures that fit around them. Because my grandfather hated his false teeth, which he called his "choppers," he kept them in the top pocket of his coveralls, hanging out just enough so that he could grab them in case he needed to chew something. He had a habit of sucking his lips inside his eyeteeth so it sort of looked like he had fangs. But Grandpa did not care what anyone looked like. His value system was based on hard work and honesty.

Every day he and I would go to the hardware store to buy stuff to fix up the old houses. I would run to our house, stick my head in the door and yell, *"I'm going with Grandpa to the hardware store!"*

My mother would always shout back, *"Don't you dare ask your grandfather to buy you anything! Do you hear me, Christopher John?"* (My name is not Christopher or John, but for some reason my mother called me that anytime she was trying to emphasize that she was serious.)

"I won't!" I would yell back. The truth is that I never had to ask; Grandpa bought me something every time we went to the store.

On its way out of the yard, the old Ford would slowly be rolling backward as I grabbed the passenger door handle and jumped inside. It was my grandfather's way of letting me know that he did not like to wait on anyone or have his time wasted. He called lazy people bums, which was about as low-life as a person could get from his perspective.

I recall one time in particular at the hardware store when Grandpa said, "Go ahead and look around. I'll find you when I'm done getting these plumbing parts."

I gravitated over to the tool aisle and became mesmerized by the hammers hanging on the gray pegboard. I stood there for a long time, staring at the tools.

Grandpa walked up and said, "Hey, knucklehead, you want one of them hammers?"

"Ah . . . no, it's okay," I replied reluctantly.

"Did your mother tell you not to ask for anything?" he said, acting slightly annoyed.

"Yeah!" I said sheepishly.

"Hurry up and pick out one of them hammers," he replied, as if he were letting my mother know who was boss.

When we got home, I ran into the house to show my mother my brand-new blue-handled Stanley hammer. "Look what Grandpa bought me!" I said, holding it up.

"Christopher John! Did you ask your grandfather for that hammer?" she asked sternly.

"Nope! He just bought it for me without asking! Honestly, I didn't ask. Really, Mom, I didn't," I said convincingly. (Looking back, I am sure my mother knew that my grandfather loved to buy me things. I think she just felt bad that we were poor, and she did not want her father to think we were trying to take advantage of his kindness.)

For two days I hammered every nail that I could find on those old houses. Finally, I got so bored pounding nails that I decided to build a go-kart. I searched everywhere for some wood. As I milled around the garage, I suddenly realized that the outside wall of my grandfather's shop was constructed of boards that were shiplapped together to create siding. I grabbed my brand-new blue Stanley hammer and began to pull the boards loose from the studs until I could not reach any higher. Then I went to the garage and took the wheels off the lawn mower. I spent most of the afternoon nailing the boards together in some semblance of a go-kart. When I was done with the frame, I took some long spikes and drove them through the center hole of the tires, attaching them to my racer.

I had just finished building my racer when my mother got home from work. She got out of her car and stood there just staring at it with a bewildered look on her face. After what seemed like an eternity, she asked hesitantly, "Christopher John, where in the world did you get that wood?"

Pointing toward the shop, I answered sheepishly, "From . . . the . . . garage . . ." Light filled the entire shop as the sun shone through the studs of the missing boards.

In a rage, Mom grabbed me by the neck and yelled, *"And where did you get those wheels?"*

"From . . . the . . . lawn mower . . ." I squeaked out, tears rolling down my cheeks.

"Your grandfather is going to kill you! Do you understand me? Your grandfather is going to kill you!" she shouted. *"Go to your room until he gets home!"*

About an hour later, I heard the '53 Ford roll up in the driveway. My heart began to pound as I heard the sound of heavy footsteps coming toward my room. My mother grabbed me by the neck and marched me out to meet my grandfather.

Squeezing my neck harder, she demanded, "Tell your grandfather what you did!"

Hanging my head in shame, I said, "I built a go-kart."

Grandpa walked over to my cobbled-together racer and smiled. "That's really cool!" he commented. Then he asked, "Where did you get the wood?"

"I got it . . . it came from the garage . . . sort of," I answered, motioning toward the shop.

When Grandpa saw the sun shining through the side of the wall, he laughed!

"Well, I guess we'll have to go get some plywood and sheet that wall. Where did you get those wheels?" he asked, still chuckling.

Feeling a bit of relief, I sighed, "From the lawn mower . . ."

"Come on, jump in the car. Hurry up, you knucklehead, and let's go get you some axles and real wheels for your race car," he said, shaking his head and chuckling some more.

When I got in the old Ford, I looked back at my mother. She was staring hard at me, as if to say, "You should've gotten a beating. Your grandfather spoils you, you little brat!"

I learned from my grandfather that when someone believes in you before you deserve it, it transforms you.

Life on the Farm

A few years later, my grandfather and grandmother bought a farm in Oakdale, California. I lived with them every summer in my teenage years and worked on the farm. Grandpa built me an awesome tree house in a huge oak tree next to the side of the hill in the orchard. It had a roof, a drawbridge to the hill, and it even had a toilet . . . of sorts. You would not really want to be under it when someone flushed their doo-doo, but it was still the coolest tree house I had ever seen. Then the next year, Grandpa bought me a brand-new red Honda 90 trail bike for Christmas.

My grandfather worked for the Hershey factory in town. He would leave me a long list of chores to accomplish while he was at work. When I was done, I was allowed to ride my motorcycle or just mess around on the farm. One day after finishing my chores, I was hanging out in my tree house and I noticed a nearby tree had recently grown through the side of it, so I decided to pull it out with my motorcycle. I grabbed about forty feet of chain, wrapped it around the intruding tree trunk and secured the other end to my motorcycle. Revving the engine, *vroom, vroooom,* I dropped it into gear and took off. The next thing I remember was flying over the handlebars, landing in the dirt. Furious with my situation, I walked up to the tree as if it were a person and said, "Tree, you've messed with the wrong guy!"

I sped back up the hill as fast as my Honda 90 would take me . . . spewing obscenities as I rode. Running into the shop, I gathered all the chain I could find. I looped it several times around my neck (I looked like Rambo) and raced back down to my tree house. I figured I needed some leverage, so I climbed to the top of the tree, dragging the chain with me. I secured the chain to the top of the tree, quickly made my way back down to the motorcycle and hooked the chain to the frame. I wanted to get up as much speed as possible, so I dragged the motorcycle over a hundred feet backward up the hill. I jumped on the bike, twisting the handle to full throttle. The engine wound tight as I shifted through the gears . . . first gear . . . second gear . . . third gear. As I hit fourth gear, I passed the tree on my right. I was going full speed. The chain grew taut, forcing the tree to the ground. Time stood still as the Honda slammed to a sudden halt, throwing me a long way from the cycle! I landed on my back just in time to see the motorcycle catapulting about a hundred feet into the air. I can still remember the sound—*Snap!* . . . *Voom!* . . . *Whoosh!* The bike flew, finally coming to rest at the top of the hill.

Out of my mind with rage, I screamed at the tree, "*You're coming down!*" I marched to the top of the hill and started up my grandfather's tractor, driving wildly down the dirt road to the tree house. (I was not supposed to use the tractor unless my grandfather was with me, but I knew he would understand that this was an emergency. No low-life, tree house–invading willow should be allowed to stand proudly in the face of a Vallotton.) I positioned the front forks of the tractor on both sides of the tree. Then I wrapped the chain around the tree, binding it tightly to the forks. I jumped onto the seat of the tractor and floored the accelerator. The engine revved so high that the fenders and hood vibrated wildly. At that moment, I pulled the hydraulic lever, forcing the front forks upward. The chain slammed tight, but the tree refused to yield. Suddenly, to my utter shock, the front forks bent straight down to the ground!

Immediately, I was back in my right mind. I unhooked the chain and slowly drove the tractor back up the hill and parked it in the barn. "*Grandpa is going to kill me! What an idiot I am! Grandpa is going to kill me! I am so dead!*" I kept repeating to myself over and over.

Minutes seemed like hours as I waited for my grandfather to get home from Hershey's. Finally, I heard the old Ford making its way toward the farmhouse. Sweat poured off my head as the car rolled to a stop. Grandpa got out and waddled over toward me.

"How was your day, knucklehead?" he teased.

"Ah . . . it was okay," I said, trying to hide my panic.

"Did you get all your stuff done?" he asked, probing.

"Yeah, I got it done . . . sort of," I responded, tearing up.

"Are you okay, Kris? Is there something bothering you, son?" he pressed.

"I'm fine . . . kind of . . . No! Actually I, sort of, really badly screwed up!"

He tilted his head as if to say, *What have you done?* I motioned to him to follow me into the barn. The forks of the tractor rested straight down on the floor of the shop. Grandpa walked slowly around the front of the tractor, carefully surveying the damage. My heart was pounding in my chest as our eyes met.

"Knucklehead, how did you bend the forks on the tractor?" he asked matter-of-factly.

I explained to him the war I had waged against the tree and my mission to extract it. He smiled as I recounted my antics.

"I've wanted to teach you how to use the torches for a while now, so this is a great opportunity for you to learn. Grab the torches and let's get this thing fixed," he said as he turned away, chuckling.

I was beginning to learn from my grandfather that love covers a multitude of sins and that I was more important to him than his stuff.

The Old Flatbed

My grandmother and grandfather came from Spain. In a Spanish family, the elders are always honored. All the family members would visit them on key holidays like Thanksgiving or Christmas to pay their respects. Of course, my grandmother would make a huge meal and insist that everybody stay and celebrate.

When I was fifteen and living on my grandfather's farm, the entire family came over for Thanksgiving. They were not Christians, so they were all drinking too much and partying. Seven of my teenage girl cousins were there with their parents. My grandfather grabbed the keys to the 1950 Dodge two-ton flatbed truck and said, "Take these keys to the old truck and give your cousins a ride through the orchard."

"Okay!" I agreed.

My preppie, city-girl cousins all jumped on the back of the truck.

"Hang on!" I said, showing off.

We blew through the orchard like a man on fire as the girls held tightly to the rusty old truck. Dust covered us as we rumbled through the orchard. Suddenly, we were stuck in a bunch of mud.

"Girls, get off and push!" I demanded.

"No way! I'm not getting dirty," one of them said.

"Me neither," the others protested.

"Come on, just push for a minute! You'll be fine," I insisted.

Still grumbling, the girls slid off the back and began to shove. I revved the motor and dumped the clutch. The dual wheels created a rooster tail twenty feet high that covered my cousins with mud as the old Dodge inched forward, finally freeing itself from the muck.

"*Jump on!*" I shouted, laughing to myself.

Yelling and screaming, the girls ran to catch the moving truck.

Encompassed in a cloud of dust again, we raced through the orchard. Climbing a six-foot ridge, we crashed onto a narrow dirt road that followed a winding river that lay some fifty feet below. I mashed the accelerator to the floor and the truck lurched forward. The flathead V-8 screamed in distress as I wound it tight before shifting it into each gear. The truck vibrated and rattled violently as it gained speed—30, 35, 40, 45, 50 mph. Dodging potholes and washouts, I fought the huge steering wheel to keep the old rig on the dirt road. Peering into the rearview mirror, I could see the girls hanging on with all their might to the plywood side rails. Suddenly, I realized that the road was completely washed out about 60 yards ahead of us. I slammed on the brakes, and we slid to a stop at the edge of the ravine. The girls crashed into the back of the cab with a thud. With the river on one side of the road and a cliff on the other, there was no way to turn around. We would have to back up three miles to the orchard.

"Open the door and make sure we don't fall off the cliff on your side," I ordered my cousin Denise, who was riding shotgun.

By now the girls in back were screaming, *"Stop! Let us off the truck! We want to walk!"*

Ignoring their pleas, I turned my head, peering through the tiny rear window. Revving the engine, I forced the shifter into reverse. The gears ground mercilessly, *Grrrr-bang!* The old rig jerked backward as the transmission finally meshed. The truck groaned in agony as we sped backward at full speed. All of a sudden, I heard a huge *Crash! Rip! Snap!* I glanced over to the passenger's side just in time to see a big tree rip the entire door off the truck. I slammed on the brakes and we skidded to a stop, but it was too late—the damage was done. The door, bent completely in half, barely hung from its lower hinge.

Horrified, Denise started screaming, "*You idiot! What are you doing? Your grandfather is going to KILL YOU!*"

By now the rest of my cousins were shouting similar obscenities at me.

We crept slowly back to the farmhouse, where the party was in full swing. I parked the truck a ways from the house.

"Don't tell anyone *we* wrecked the truck," I ordered.

"What?" they protested. "*You* crashed the truck, not us!"

Still covered in mud, they ran toward the party and yelled, "*Kris wrecked the truck! Kris destroyed the truck!*"

Two of my uncles (fathers of the girls) came rushing out. Eyeing what was left of the passenger door, they came toward me, ranting in a loud voice, "What did you do this time? Are you some kind of nut? You could have killed those girls!" (Meanwhile, my cousins were snickering and laughing in the background.)

Just then, my grandfather waddled up and demanded to know what happened.

"Sparky [my grandfather's nickname], this idiot grandson of yours wrecked the farm truck and almost killed the girls!" they told him.

My grandfather looked up at me as if to say, *Don't speak. I've got this handled.* I stood there quietly, choking back tears, as my grandfather assessed the damage.

"Oh," he said confidently, "it's just the door. I've wanted to take both doors off that old farm truck for quite some time. . . . I just never got around to it. Opening and closing those doors is a big waste of time! Kris, grab some tools and take both doors off," he ordered with a wink.

My uncles were livid! They continued yelling and screaming, until finally my grandfather had heard enough.

197

Interrupting them, he said, "The boy has work to do. Leave him alone!"

Although my grandfather was an atheist until the year before he died, he taught me more about the love of God than anyone else in the world. He adored me in spite of my blunders. He never made me feel like the rules were more important than our relationship. He often corrected me, but he refused to punish me. I actually believe that my grandfather knew more about love before he met Christ than most mature believers know. His ability to love me unconditionally transformed my life. It was his "felt love" for me that kept me from turning to drugs and alcohol in those tough teenage years.

Sacrifice and Passion

A lot of things masquerade as love, but are really just cheap imitations of the real thing. Reproductions often look noble on the outside, but they lead to deep vortexes of emptiness and bondage. True freedom only occurs when we break off the shackles of fear and embrace a culture of mercy and grace. I am sure my uncles had righteous motivation for wanting to whip me, yet punishing people for their mistakes creates self-destructive ecosystems that invite demonic oppression.

On the other hand, true love eradicates fear, which inoculates us from punishment. Remember John's exhortation I quoted at the beginning of this chapter? He wrote that perfect love casts out fear, because fear involves punishment. That is why the entire Gospel can be boiled down to *loving God and loving each other*.

Synthetic imitations of love have many faces, but the most common alias is sacrifice. The Bible says, "If I give all my possessions to feed the poor, and if I surrender my body to be burned, but do not have love, it profits me nothing" (1 Corinthians 13:3). It is important to understand that we can sacrifice, yet not love! Many people exchange sacrifice for love. These people measure the depth of their spirituality by the list of disciplines and tough ministry situations that they *do* for God. They are deceived into believing that sacrifice gives them favor with Jesus.

A long time ago, my good friend John had an encounter with God that drove this point home for me. John had disciplined himself to spend long periods of time in prayer and worship. Whenever he would fail to meet his goal, he would feel guilty and spend several hours repenting. Finally, one day God had had enough of John's efforts. He said to him, *John, I want to be your friend, not your habit!*

My grandfather loved me just because he did . . . it was not duty or habit. It was honestly love in his heart. He did not have to feel it, fake it or do anything to prove it. He just did. He built a tree house for me and helped me with my stuff, but honestly, what I remember the most is that he believed in me and had passion for me. I understand that the world has replaced love with lust, so talking about *passion* inspires visions of pornography or perversion. But true love arouses passion in the true sense of the word, which results in enthusiasm, excitement and zeal.

It is time for Jesus to kiss His Bride awake! The hollowed out, Spock-like Vulcan Christianity must give way to heart-felt, risk-filled love for God and for people. Heidi and Rolland Baker gave up a life of luxury to sit in the dirt with kids in the jungles of Africa. Heidi has a Ph.D., and Rolland has a genius IQ. People who do not know them well often talk to me about the Bakers' sacrifice. It is true that they have lain down their lives for God, but they did not go to Africa just to suffer for Jesus. We are intimate friends with them and have spent hours talking about their ministry. Whenever the subject of reaching the poor or transforming Africa comes up, their eyes light up, the tone of their voice changes and excitement begins to gush out of them like a wild river. Like my grandfather, they love people! They love them just because they do. They are not trying to win some special place with God or impress the masses. They just cannot help themselves. They are possessed with passion; it oozes out of them. (Passion always looks like sacrifice to people who are not in love.)

When passion possesses us, our hearts are swept clean and our souls are full of life. It does not matter if seven or seventy evil spirits return to try to take up residence—there is no room for them! The place is so packed with power that it seeps from every crack in the wall! Passion will cause us to live in places that sacrifice could only die for.

Speaking of passion, I mentioned at the start that I met Kathy when we were just kids, but I decided the day I met her that I had to have her. As I told you earlier, we lived thirty miles apart. My little Honda motorcycle was too small to ride on the freeway, so I took an hour-and-a-half journey on back roads to see her. It did not matter if it was pouring rain or freezing cold—I had to see my baby! I would often arrive at her house soaked to my underwear, my face blue and my hands stiff from the cold. But in the five years we dated, I never missed a single weekend.

Nobody ever sat me down and said, "Kris, if you really love this woman, you will have to lay down your life for her." Those words are for people who have lost their passion, whose houses may be swept clean, yet they remain unfurnished, empty echoes of hollow love . . . clouds without rain.

Lovers just love—it is in their bones—they cannot help it. But true love must also be cultivated in our lives or soon the fire goes out and our relationships are reduced to duty and sacrifice. King Solomon and his Shulammite bride are great examples of people who cultivated their love for one another. Reading their love letter makes you want to blush and say, "Hey, guys, get a room!" Let's look at a few of the exchanges between Solomon and his bride.

The Shulammite Bride

May he kiss me with the kisses of his mouth!
For your love is better than wine.
Song of Solomon 1:2

Listen! My beloved!
Behold, he is coming,
Climbing on the mountains,
Leaping on the hills!
My beloved is like a gazelle or a young stag.
Behold, he is standing behind our wall,
He is looking through the windows,
He is peering through the lattice.
Song of Solomon 2:8–9

I must arise now and go about the city;
In the streets and in the squares
I must seek him whom my soul loves.
Song of Solomon 3:2

Solomon the Bridegroom

How beautiful you are, my darling,
How beautiful you are!
Your eyes are like doves behind your veil;
Your hair is like a flock of goats
That have descended from Mount Gilead.
Your teeth are like a flock of newly shorn ewes
Which have come up from their washing,
All of which bear twins,
And not one among them has lost her young.
Your lips are like a scarlet thread,
And your mouth is lovely.
Your temples are like a slice of a pomegranate
Behind your veil.
Your neck is like the tower of David,
Built with rows of stones
On which are hung a thousand shields,
All the round shields of the mighty men.
Your two breasts are like two fawns,
Twins of a gazelle
Which feed among the lilies.
Until the cool of the day
When the shadows flee away,
I will go my way to the mountain of myrrh
And to the hill of frankincense.
You are altogether beautiful, my darling,
And there is no blemish in you.

Song of Solomon 4:1–7

This is passionate stuff! (I tried some of that "your neck is like a tower and your teeth are like a flock of goats" stuff with Kathy, and it did not go over so well. I think you have to use some different words.) I have been with Kathy for more than forty years, and the one thing our marriage has never been is boring. Living life passionately together is an adventure. I do, however, wonder what it would be like to be as rich as Solomon and his bride, who had choirs following them around all day singing love songs to them!

The world is looking for something worth dying for so that they have something really worth living for. Life has gotten so boring for most people that they have become mesmerized with television and movies. Many people spend their days sitting in front of the tube, waiting for life to start. Their passion is siphoned off as they mindlessly stare at some actor or actress living out a reality they long to have themselves. I do not know who coined the statement "an idle mind is the devil's playground," but it is true. When camping in dangerous places, it is often recommended that you keep a campfire going to keep the predators away. When we set our hearts on fire, demonic predators stay out of our camp, which is my main point in this chapter.

The apostle Paul put it best: "Love never fails" (see 1 Corinthians 13:8). We have spent several chapters talking about how to win spiritual battles in our own lives and in the lives of others. But when all else fails, remember this: Love cannot be defeated. There is no prison so secure that love cannot free you. There is no captor so strong that love cannot liberate you. There is no sin so terrible that love cannot restore you. Real love is a secret weapon that our enemy has no answer for. Whenever we roll it out on the battlefield, Satan falls like lightning.

May love fill us, the Holy Spirit lead us and the Father embrace us. It is time to really live again!

Notes

Chapter 5: The Flesh Is Weak

1. Kris Vallotton and Jason Vallotton, *The Supernatural Power of Forgiveness: Discover How to Escape Your Prison of Pain and Unlock a Life of Freedom* (Ventura, Calif.: Regal, 2011).

2. Kris Vallotton, *Developing a Supernatural Lifestyle: A Practical Guide to a Life of Signs, Wonders, and Miracles* (Shippensburg, Penn.: Destiny Image, 2007).

3. Lucinda Bassett, *From Panic to Power: Proven Techniques to Calm Your Anxieties, Conquer Your Fears, and Put You in Control of Your Life* (New York: Harper, 1996).

4. Caroline Leaf, Ph.D., *Who Switched Off My Brain? Controlling Toxic Thoughts and Emotions* (Nashville: Thomas Nelson, 2009).

Chapter 6: Treating Yourself Kindly

1. Bill Johnson and Kris Vallotton, *The Supernatural Ways of Royalty: Discovering Your Rights and Privileges of Being a Son or Daughter of God* (Shippensburg, Penn.: Destiny Image, 2009).

2. Bill Johnson, *Strengthen Yourself in the Lord: How to Release the Hidden Power of God in Your Life* (Shippensburg, Penn.: Destiny Image, 2007).

Chapter 7: Serious Joy

1. Norman Cousins, *Anatomy of an Illness* (New York: W.W. Norton & Company, 1979), 43.

2. Michelle W. Murray, "Laughter Is the 'Best Medicine' For Your Heart," (July 14, 2009), http://www.umm.edu/features/laughter.htm.

3. Marshall Brain, "How Laughter Works," (April 01, 2000), http://health.howstuffworks.com/mental-health/human-nature/other-emotions/laughter.htm.

4. Paul McGhee, Ph.D., *Humor: The Lighter Path to Resilience and Health* (Bloomington, Ind.: AuthorHouse, 2010), 82.

5. Robert Provine, "The Science of Laughter," http://www.psychologytoday.com/articles/200011/the-science-laughter.

6. Madan Kataria, *Laugh for No Reason* (Bengaluru, India: Madhuri International, 1999).

Chapter 8: The Armor of God

1. Kris Vallotton, *Heavy Rain: Renew the Church, Transform the World* (Ventura, Calif.: Regal, 2010).

About the Author

Kris and Kathy Vallotton have been happily married for 36 years. They have four children and eight grandchildren. Three of their children are in full-time vocational ministry. Kris is the cofounder and senior overseer of the Bethel School of Supernatural Ministry, which has grown to more than thirteen hundred full-time students in thirteen years. He is also the founder and president of Moral Revolution, an organization dedicated to cultural transformation.

Kris is the senior associate leader of Bethel Church in Redding, California, and has served with Bill Johnson for more than 33 years. He has written six other books, including the bestselling *Heavy Rain* and also *The Supernatural Ways of Royalty* (co-authored with Bill Johnson). Kris's revelatory insight and humorous delivery make him a much sought-after international conference speaker.

You can contact Kris or find out more about his other ministry materials at www.kvministries.com, or you can follow Kris and Kathy on their Facebook fan page at www.facebook.com/kvministries.

Other Books by Kris Vallotton

Developing a Supernatural Lifestyle: A Practical Guide to a Life of Signs, Wonders, and Miracles

Heavy Rain: Renew the Church, Transform the World

Moral Revolution: The Naked Truth about Sexual Purity

The Supernatural Power of Forgiveness: Discover How to Escape Your Prison of Pain and Unlock a Life of Freedom (co-authored with Jason Vallotton)

The Supernatural Ways of Royalty: Discovering Your Rights and Privileges of Being a Son or Daughter of God (co-authored with Bill Johnson)

Basic Training for the Supernatural Ways of Royalty (workbook)

Basic Training for the Prophetic Ministry (workbook)